Serious
Leisure

A Perspective for Our Time

Serious Leisure

Robert A. Stebbins

Transaction Publishers

New Brunswick (U.S.A.) and London (U.K.)

306.4812
S81s

Copyright © 2007 by Transaction Publishers, New Brunswick, New Jersey.

All rights reserved under International and Pan-American Copyright Conventions. No part of this book may be reproduced or transmitted in any form or by any means, electronic or mechanical, including photocopy, recording, or any information storage and retrieval system, without prior permission in writing from the publisher. All inquiries should be addressed to Transaction Publishers, Rutgers—The State University, 35 Berrue Circle, Piscataway, New Jersey 08854-8042. www.transactionpub.com

This book is printed on acid-free paper that meets the American National Standard for Permanence of Paper for Printed Library Materials.

Library of Congress Catalog Number: 2006050176
ISBN: 0-7658-0363-1
       978-0-7658-0363-4
Printed in the United States of America

Library of Congress Cataloging-in-Publication Data

Stebbins, Robert A., 1938-
  Serious leisure : a perspective for our time / Robert A. Stebbins.
        p. cm.
  Includes bibliographical references and index.
  ISBN 0-7658-0363-1 (alk. paper)
  1. Leisure—Sociological aspects. I. Title.

GV14.45.S843 2006
306.4'—dc22   20006050176

To Abran, Amélie, Braeden, and Landon

University Libraries
Carnegie Mellon University
Pittsburgh, PA 15213-3890

BLEST, who can unconcernedly find hours, days and years, slide soft away, in health of body, peace of mind, quiet of day, should sleep by night, study and ease, together mixed—sweet recreation.

"Ode on Solitude"
by Alexander Pope (1717)

Contents

List of Tables and Figures

Preface

This book was, in part, born of the necessity to gather the widely scattered literature on serious and casual leisure into a single handy, coherent, comprehensive resource. My scholarly involvements as participant at conferences, speaker on university campuses, evaluator of manuscripts, supervisor of graduate students, and e-mail mentor have, together, made me increasingly aware of the need for such a volume. More and more, I discovered that people are overlooking critical parts of the Perspective, and sometimes blaming it (and me) for being shortsighted in those ways. It is not that the Perspective is above reproach. This book candidly shows many of its weaknesses and limitations. Rather it is that so much has now been written in its name and published in so great a variety of outlets that fewer and fewer people are able to see the entire picture.

To start with, then, this book constitutes a stocktaking of the literature on serious literature, the third such effort. The second occurred in 1999-2000 and was published in New Directions in the Theory and Research on Serious Leisure (Stebbins, 2001a) and the first occurred in 1990-1991, which was then published in Amateurs, Professionals, and Serious Leisure (Stebbins, 1992a). This, the third stocktaking, has been revealing, in that approximately one and one-half times as much was published since the 1999-2000 stocktaking in approximately half the time. This trend, in itself, justifies this book.

But, in fact, this book is far more than just another stocktaking, however greatly needed such a service. For the book is, most centrally, about three forms of leisure synthesized into a common perspective. Serious leisure is but one of these forms, the other two being casual leisure and project-based leisure. Together they comprise the serious leisure perspective. This title may alarm some readers, but they should read the first paragraph of chapter 1 for an explanation. This Perspective can be defined simply as the theoretic framework that synthesizes three main forms of leisure showing, at once, their distinctive features, similarities, and interrelationships.

The three are briefly defined as follows:

- Serious leisure: systematic pursuit of an amateur, hobbyist, or volunteer core activity sufficiently substantial, interesting. and fulfilling in nature for the participant to find a career there acquiring and expressing a combination of its special skills, knowledge, and experience
- Casual leisure: immediately, intrinsically rewarding, relatively short-lived pleasurable core activity, requiring little or no special training to enjoy it.
- Project-based leisure: short-term, reasonably complicated, one-shot or occasional, though infrequent, creative undertaking carried out in free time, or time free of disagreeable obligation.

Although it was never my intention as I moved over the years from one study of free-time activity to another, my findings and theoretic musings have nevertheless evolved and coalesced into a typological map of the world of leisure. That is, so far as I can tell at present, all leisure (at least in Western society) can be classified according to one of the three forms and their several types and subtypes. More precisely the serious leisure perspective offers a classification and explanation of all leisure activity and experience, as these two are framed in the social psychological, social, cultural, and historical contexts in which the activity and experience take place.

On the way to this synthesis I set out in chapters 1 and 3 the basic concepts and propositions that make up the three forms. My goal here is to focus attention on their essential elements. The stocktaking of the serious leisure literature is carried out in chapter 2, while that for casual and project-based leisure, a much smaller undertaking, is left for chapter 3. I then present in chapter 4 the synthesis itself. It is realized by way of a set of foundational concepts—organization, community, history, lifestyle, and culture—and several of their component areas. Chapter 5 is devoted to extending the perspective, now reasonably synthesized, into other disciplines and fields of research. Sixteen such extensions are described, along with some additional ones that are, so to speak, waiting to be formally recognized through publication. In chapter 6 we look at the history of the Perspective, starting in early 1974 with serious leisure and then adding historical commentary on, first, casual leisure and, then, project-based leisure. Chapter 7 centers on the future and importance of the serious leisure perspective, its place in a globalizing world, and some of its critical links with other fields of knowledge and practice, notably the nonprofit sector and preventive medicine.

My hope in writing this book is that many more people than presently around will wake up to the fact that leisure, even if some of it is trivial, is not, as a whole and as a phenomenon in the twenty-first century, a trivial matter. The study of serious leisure roots, in part, in the failure of modern sociologists to view leisure as a distinctive aspect of society and social life. In 1974, I could find no sociological definition of amateur or hobbyist and no recognition in sociology (the discipline I was trained in) of the unique role and status played by those who pursue amateur and hobbyist activities. Regrettably not much has changed since that year. To be sure, the occasional leisure-oriented article is published in the sociological journals, but institutional sociology still mostly ignores this area of social life. For example one hunts in vain for a session on leisure at a typical annual meeting of the American Sociological Association or the Canadian Sociology and Anthropology Association. And it is Mission Impossible trying to find leisure listed as an area of specialization in the graduate programs in sociology offered in North American universities. And the latter situation is hardly surprising: virtually no faculty member in these programs has been trained in the sociology of leisure. It is the chicken and the egg.

Yet the sociology of leisure is alive and well, albeit living in academic locations far a field from sociology departments. In units variously named Leisure Studies, Leisure and Recreation, Leisure and Physical Education, Parks and Leisure, and more recently, Leisure and Health Studies, the sociology of leisure has grown into a vibrant branch of knowledge. So it is not really that branch of the discipline which is weak, rather weakness lies within the discipline itself. It is weak because it is ignoring a side of social life that society itself takes very seriously, spends a great deal of money on, and, for much of that society, sets its sights on. Sayings like "thank God it's Friday" and "all work and no play makes Jack [and Jane] a dull boy" should be pondered more closely by sociology as a discipline.

This book, offering as it does, an organized and coherent view of a large segment of the scholarly side of the sociology of leisure, might just be what it takes to get sociology back on track in a field that it helped pioneer. Does anyone remember Veblen, Lundberg, Hollingshead, and Riesman?

Acknowledgements

First, many thanks to Mary Thompson of the University of Lethbridge who most convincingly put the bug in my ear that an idea like the serious leisure perspective was valid, important, and therefore in need of cultivating. As she taught her initial undergraduate class on serious leisure, we both came to realize that this conceptual story was, in fact, impossible to tell properly without substantial mention of the other two forms. Mary taught in winter term 2005. In August that year Jenna Hartel and I met by chance in an elevator at the annual meeting of the American Sociological Association. Pen pals for at least a year, owing to her own interest in serious leisure and information science, she subsequently observed that the first should have its own website and that she would be willing to help me develop it. That possibility galvanized me into action: the website should be about the entire Perspective, not only about its namesake. But, to have an effective site, it was first required that I write this book. The site (www.soci.ucalgary.ca/seriousleisure) was officially launched in early April 2006, and is closely coordinated with these pages.

Finally, the editorial assistance of Laurence Mintz was, as always, of excellent quality. I deeply appreciate his contributions to this book.

1

The Serious Leisure Perspective

The phrase "serious leisure perspective" is my name for the theoretic framework that synthesizes three main forms of leisure, known as *serious leisure*, *casual leisure*, and *project-based leisure*. Research began early in 1974 on the first of these, and has continued since that time, while work on casual leisure and then on project-based leisure came subsequently. Within each form a variety of types and subtypes has also emerged over the years. That the Perspective (wherever Perspective appears as shorthand for serious leisure perspective, to avoid confusion, the first letter will be capitalized) takes its name from the first of these should, in no way, suggest that I regard it, in some abstract sense, as the most important or superior of the three. I hope the following pages will demonstrate the folly of that kind of thinking. Rather the Perspective is so titled, simply because it got its start in the study of serious leisure; such leisure is, strictly from the standpoint of intellectual invention, the godfather of the other two.

Furthermore serious leisure has become the benchmark from which analyses of casual and project-based leisure have often been undertaken. So naming the Perspective after the first facilitates intellectual recognition; it keeps the idea in familiar territory for all concerned. Be that as it may, I might have titled it "core activity perspective," for all three forms are labels for kinds of distinctive sets of interrelated actions or steps that must be followed to achieve an outcome or product that the participant finds attractive. For instance, in serious leisure, a core activity of alpine skiing is descending snow-covered slopes, that of cabinet making is shaping and finishing wood, and that of volunteer fire fighting is putting out blazes and rescuing people from them. In each case, the participant takes several interrelated steps to successfully ski down hill, make a cabinet, or rescue someone. In casual leisure core activities, which are much less complex than in serious leisure, are exemplified in the actions required

1

to hold sociable conversations with friends, savor beautiful scenery, and offer simple volunteer services (e.g., handing out leaflets, directing traffic in a parking lot, clearing snow off the neighborhood hockey rink). In leisure projects, core activities are intense, though limited in time and moderate in complexity, as seen in the actions of serving as scorekeeper during an amateur sports tournament or serving as museum guide during a special exhibition of artifacts. Engaging in the core activity (and its component steps and actions) is a main feature that attracts participants to the leisure in question and encourages them to return for more. In short the core activity is a value in its own right, even if more strongly held for some leisure activities than others.

Similarly, I might have dubbed this framework the "leisure experience perspective." After all each of the three forms refers to an identifiable kind of experience had during free time. Indeed, it fits all three of Mannell's (1999) conceptualizations of this experience, as subjectively defined leisure, as immediate conscious experience, and as post hoc satisfaction.

Still this label would be too limiting, for the Perspective is broader than what people experience in their leisure. It also provides a way of looking on the social, cultural, and historical context of that experience. A similar problem undermines the suggestion made by Tomlinson (1993) that serious leisure be called "committed leisure." Though we shall see later in this chapter that commitment is certainly an important attitude in serious leisure, it is, nevertheless, too narrow to serve as a descriptor of the latter. Moreover, the other two forms in the Perspective also generate commitment on occasion.

Because the serious and casual forms have sometimes stirred discussion about the relative merit of one or the other, let us be clear from the outset that the serious leisure perspective looks on each as important in its own way. That is, it is much less a question of which is best, than a question of how well combinations of two or three of the forms serve individuals, categories of individuals (e.g., sex, age, social class, religion, nationality), and their larger communities and societies. This, in turn, leads to such considerations as leisure lifestyle, optimal leisure lifestyle, and social capital, all of which are, themselves, important concepts in this framework.

The idea of perspective communicates at least three important points. One, any perspective is a way of theoretically viewing leisure phenomena. So, this one, too, provides a unique prism through which to look at what people do in their free time. Two, as a theoretic framework, the serious leisure perspective synthesizes the three forms, showing at once their distinctive features, their similarities, and their interrelationships. Three, although it was never my intention as I moved from one study of free-time activity to the next, my findings and theoretic musings have nevertheless evolved into a typological map of the world of leisure. That is, so far as I can tell at present, all leisure (at least in Western society) can be classified according to one of the three forms. But, consistent with the exploratory approach that has guided much of basic research in this field, open-ended inquiry and observation could, some day, suggest one or more additional forms. Briefly put the construction of scientific typologies, in principle, never results in completed intellectual edifices.

Additionally the serious leisure perspective is the product of extensive exploratory research (Glaser and Strauss, 1967; Stebbins, 2001c), some of it more systematic, some of it less so. In general, it may be said that it arose directly from open-ended observations or interviews, often both, conducted on a wide range of leisure activities. Today the serious leisure perspective is, in the words of Glaser and Strauss, a "formal grounded theory." Moreover, as such it is no longer strictly exploratory in scope, for as we shall see from time to time, considerable confirmatory work has now been carried out, work designed to add precision and detail to the basic Perspective as previously explored.

In the present chapter we take a look at the basics of serious leisure, then, in chapter 2, I review the research on serious leisure as published from, in most instances, the year 2000. In chapter 3 we look at the basics of casual and project-based leisure as well as the much sparser research that has been done in their name. In chapter 4 I fill in the Perspective, making it, as much as is possible given current knowledge, a proper synthesis of the three forms rather than a simple typology of them. This is accomplished by a process of elaboration using several concepts that find expression in each of the three forms. Chapter 5 looks at the diverse extensions of the basic Perspective into areas of life where it has already provided, or looks as though it may provide, a valid and useful explanation of human motivation, group formation, collective action, and the like. The history of the serious leisure perspective is presented in the next chapter. The final chapter explores the question of why it is necessary to classify leisure activities. It also considers how the Perspective applies outside the West, what it can offer to the world, how it relates to health and well-being as well as its place is in the nonprofit sector.

My aim in all this is to provide a stand-alone, though reasonably in-depth statement of the serious leisure perspective, which will serve both the scholarly community and the larger public who want to learn about it. But many details must necessarily be left out, for to add them, would make this book far too dense and unwieldy. To signal where this has happened, I refer from time to time, mostly in chapters 1 and 3, to sources where the subject at hand can be examined in greater detail (a bibliography, continually updated, listing all publications bearing on the Perspective is available at www.soci.ucalgary.ca/seriousleisure). Chapters 1, 3, and 4 present the serious leisure perspective, and are therefore "must reads." The other chapters are important for anyone who wants to know where this Perspective fits in the modern world.

Inasmuch as this is, at bottom, a disquisition about basics and basic concepts in leisure studies, we must of necessity open it with a definitional statement on the most fundamental of all ideas in that field, namely, leisure itself.

A Definition of Leisure

Starting with Aristotle, scholars, clergy, and journalists, among other categories of humankind, have been weighing in with their definitions of leisure. Given the scope of this book, it is unnecessary to review these conceptualizations. Rather what is called for in this book is a working definition of the concept that respects their insights into such activity, but that also logically fits the serious leisure perspective, while demarcating clearly the sphere of human life to which it applies. To this end, leisure is defined here as: uncoerced activity engaged in during free time, which people want to do and, in either a satisfying or a fulfilling way (or both), use their abilities and resources to succeed at this. "Free time" is time away from unpleasant obligation, with pleasant obligation being treated here as essentially leisure since *homo otiosus,* leisure man, feels no significant coercion to enact the activity in question (Stebbins, 2000b).

Note that reference to "free choice"—a long-standing component of standard definitions of leisure—is for reasons discussed in detail elsewhere (Stebbins, 2005b), intentionally omitted from this definition. Generally put choice is never completely free, but rather hedged about with all sorts of conditions. This situation renders this concept and allied ones such as freedom and state of mind useless as essential elements in a basic definition (Juniu and Henderson, 2001). Note, too, there is no reference in this definition to the moral basis of leisure; that is, contrary to some stances taken in the past (e.g., Kaplan, 1960, pp. 22-25), leisure in the serious leisure perspective can be either deviant or non-deviant (see chapter 4 of the present volume).

Nor is free time treated here as synonymous with leisure. We can be bored in our free time, which can result from inactivity ("nothing to do") or from activity, which alas, is uninteresting, unstimulating. The same can, of course, happen at work and in obligated nonwork settings. Since boredom is a decidedly negative state of mind, it can be argued that, logically, it is not leisure at all. For leisure is typically conceived of as a positive mindset, composed of, among other sentiments, pleasant expectations and recollections of activities and situations. Of course, it happens at times that expectations turn out to be unrealistic, and we get bored (or perhaps angry, frightened, or embarrassed) with the activity in question, transforming it in our view into something quite other than leisure. And all this may happen in free time, which exemplifies well how such time can occupy a broader area of life than leisure, which is nested within (Stebbins, 2003a).

Serious Leisure

Serious leisure is the systematic pursuit of an amateur, hobbyist, or volunteer core activity that people find so substantial, interesting, and fulfilling that, in the typical case, they launch themselves on a (leisure) career centered on acquiring and expressing a combination of its special skills, knowledge, and experience (modified from Stebbins, 1992, p. 3). Serious leisure has been typically contrasted with "casual" or "unserious" leisure, which is considerably less substantial and offers no career of the sort just described. It is defined as an immediately, intrinsically rewarding, relatively short-lived pleasurable core activity, requiring little or no special training to enjoy it (Stebbins, 1997a, p. 18). Although I once viewed casual leisure as residual, as all leisure falling outside the three main types of serious leisure, this has turned out to be erroneous. For I have observed, in recent years, a third kind of leisure, namely, project-based leisure. It is a short-term, reasonably complicated, one-off or occasional, though infrequent, creative undertaking (core activity) carried out in free time, or time free of disagreeable obligation (Stebbins, 2005a; on obligation and free time, see Stebbins, 2000b).

The Basic Serious Leisure Framework

The basic framework of all three forms—serious, casual, and project-based leisure—is made up of the central defining concepts that help distinguish each form from the other two and from related concepts in adjacent fields of research. These sets of concepts are, in turn, anchored in broader social contexts, which are the subject of chapter 4.

As for serious leisure, it is constituted of three types: amateur pursuits, hobbyist activities, and career volunteering. Amateurs are found in art, science, sport, and entertainment, where they are inevitably linked, one way or another, with professional counterparts who coalesce, along with the public whom the two groups share, into a three-way system of relations and relationships (the professional-amateur-public, or P-A-P, system). Earlier (e.g., Stebbins, 1992a, chap. 2) I argued that the professionals should be identified and defined according to theory developed in the sociological study of the professions, a substantially more exact procedure than the ones relying on the simplistic and not infrequently commercially shaped commonsense images of these workers. Yet, apart from me, I know of no one who has conceived of the professional counterparts of a particular group of amateurs in these sociological terms. Rather leisure studies researchers have been content to use the simpler economic definition of professional as a person who is paid for the activity in question. I now see the merit of their position, for what is important for the study of amateurs and hobbyists is that some of them begin to make some sort of living at the activity. Freed partly or wholly from having to make a living in another field, it becomes possible for these people to devote more time to their serious leisure and thus, in some instances, excel over their counterparts in leisure who can only pursue the activity after a full day's work elsewhere. That in some fields, mostly those in art, sport, science, and entertainment, sociological professionals are actually present is, in leisure studies, beside the point. That is, reaching such an advanced stage of professionalization is a concern of the sociology of work, not of the sociology of leisure.

As a result of this reasoning I now want to redefine "professional" in (economic rather than sociological) terms that relate better to amateurs and hobbyists, namely, as someone who is dependent on the income from an activity that other people pursue with little or no remuneration as leisure. The income on which the professional is dependent may be this person's only source of money (i.e., full-time professional) or it may be one of two or more sources of money (i.e., part-time professional). Although some of these professionals may be sociological professionals, as just described, many economic professionals are in fields where professionalization is only beginning.

This condition suggests a critical precaution: enactment of the core activity by the professionals in a particular field, to influence amateurs there, must be sufficiently visible to those amateurs. If the amateurs, in general, have no idea of the prowess of their professional counterparts, the latter become irrelevant as role models, and the leisure side of the activity remains at a hobbyist level. These definitional modifications retain the integrity of the earlier model, which states that amateurs and professionals are locked in and therefore further defined, in most instances, by their place in a professional-amateur-public (P-A-P) system of relations, an arrangement too complex to describe further in this book (for details see Stebbins, 1979; 1992a, pp. 38-41; 2002, pp. 129-130).

Yoder's study (1997) of tournament bass fishing in the United States engendered an important modification of the original P-A-P model. He found, first, that fishers here are amateurs, not hobbyists, and second, that commodity producers serving both amateur and professional tournament fishers play a role significant enough to warrant changing the original triangular professional-amateur-public (P-A-P) system of relationships first set out in Stebbins (1979). In other words, in the social world of these amateurs the "strangers" (Unruh, 1979) are a highly important group consisting, in the main, of national fishing organizations, tourna-ment promoters, and manufacturers and distributors of sporting goods and services. Significant numbers of amateurs make, sell, or advertise commodities for the sport. And the professional fishers are supported by the commodity agents by way of paid entry fees for tournaments, provi-sion of boats and fishing tackle, and subsidies for living expenses. Top professionals are given a salary to promote fishing commodities. Yoder's (1997, p. 416) modification results in a more complicated triangular model, consisting of a system of relationships linking commodity agents, professionals/commodity agents, and amateurs/publics (C-PC-AP).

The new C-PC-AP model sharpens our understanding of some other amateur fields as well. One of them is stand-up comedy, where the in-fluence of a manager, booking agent, or comedy club owner can weigh heavily on the career of the performer (see Stebbins, 1990, chap. 7). It is likewise for certain types of entertainment magicians and the magic deal-ers and booking agents who inhabit their social world (Stebbins, 1993a). And Wilson (1995) describes a similar, "symbiotic" relationship between British marathon runners and the media. But, for amateurs in other fields of art, science, sport, and entertainment, who are also linked to sets of strangers operating in their special social worlds, these strangers play a much more subdued role compared with the four fields just mentioned. Thus for many amateur activities, the simpler, P-A-P model still offers the most valid explanation of their social structure.

It was through the study of amateurs that I came to realize that the standard practice among sociologists of treating all professionals as of a kind was short sighted. Professionals in the arts, science, sport, and entertainment fields are quite different from those in the "professions" (e.g., law, medicine, teaching, accounting, engineering). The first set of workers may be viewed as *public-centered* and the second as *client-centered*. The first serve publics in art, sport, science, and entertainment, whereas the second serve various clients such as patients or purchasers of a highly skilled service offered by, say, a lawyer, architect, counsellor, engineer, or accountant (Stebbins, 1992a, p. 22).

Hobbyists lack the professional alter ego (as redefined above) of amateurs, although they sometimes have commercial equivalents and often have small publics who take an interest in what they do. Hobbyists are classified according to five categories: collectors, makers and tinkerers, activity participants (in noncompetitive, rule-based, pursuits such as fishing and barbershop singing), players of sports and games (in competitive, rule-based activities with no professional counterparts like long-distance running and competitive swimming) and the enthusiasts of the liberal arts hobbies. The rules guiding rule-based pursuits are, for the most part, either subcultural (informal) or regulatory (formal). Thus seasoned hikers in North America's Rocky Mountains know they should, for example, stay on established trails, pack out all garbage, be prepared for sudden changes in weather, and make noise to scare off bears.

The liberal arts hobbyists are enamored of the systematic acquisition of knowledge for its own sake. Many of them accomplish this by reading voraciously in a field of art, sport, cuisine, language, culture, history, science, philosophy, politics, or literature (Stebbins, 1994a). But some of them go beyond this to expand their knowledge still further through cultural tourism, documentary videos, television programs, and similar resources. Although the matter has yet to be studied through research, it is theoretically possible to separate buffs from consumers in the liberal arts hobbies of sport, cuisine, and the fine and entertainment arts. Some people —call them *consumers*—more or less uncritically consume restaurant fare, sports events, or displays of art (concerts, shows, exhibitions) as pure entertainment and sensory stimulation (casual leisure), whereas others —call them *buffs*—participate in these same situations as more or less knowledgeable experts, as serious leisure (for more on this distinction, see Stebbins 2002, chap. 5). The ever-rarer Renaissance man of our day may also be classified here, even though such people avoid specializing in one field of learning to acquire, instead, a somewhat more superficial knowledge of a variety of fields. Being broadly well-read is a (liberal arts) hobby of its own.

What I have come to refer to as "the nature-challenge" hobbies (Stebbins, 2005c) fall under the theoretic heading of noncompetitive, rule-based activity participation. True, actual competitions are sometimes held in, for instance, snowboarding, kayaking, and mountain biking (e.g., fastest time over a particular course), but mostly beating nature is thrill enough. Moreover, other nature hobbies exist, which are also challenging, but in very different ways. Some, most notably fishing and hunting, in essence exploit the natural environment. Still others center on appreciation of the outdoors, among them hiking, backpacking, bird watching, and horseback riding (Stebbins, 1998a, p. 59).

Turning now to volunteering, Cnaan, Handy, and Wadsworth (1996) identified four dimensions they found running throughout the several definitions of volunteering they examined. These dimensions are free choice, remuneration, structure, and intended beneficiaries. The following *volitional* definition was created from these four: volunteering is uncoerced help offered either formally or informally with no or, at most, token pay and done for the benefit of both other people (beyond the volunteer's family) and the volunteer (modified from Stebbins, 2004a, p. 5). This conception of volunteering revolves, in significant part, around a central subjective motivational question: it must be determined whether volunteers feel they are engaging in an enjoyable (casual leisure), fulfilling (serious leisure), or enjoyable or fulfilling (project-based leisure) core activity that they have had the option to accept or reject on their own terms. A key element in the leisure conception of volunteering is the felt absence of moral coercion to do the volunteer activity, an element that, in "marginal volunteering" (Stebbins, 2001d) may be experienced in degrees, as more or less coercive. Nevertheless the reigning conception of volunteering in nonprofit sector research is not that of volunteering as leisure, but volunteering as unpaid work. This *economic* conception defines volunteering as the absence of payment for a livelihood, whether in money or in kind. This definition largely avoids the messy question of motivation so crucial to the leisure conception.

Concerning the dimension of free choice, the language of (lack of) "coercion," is preferred, as indicated in the earlier section on the definition of leisure, because that of "free choice" is hedged about with numerous problems. The logical difficulties of including obligation in definitions of volunteering militate against including this condition in the foregoing definition (see Stebbins, 2001d). As for remuneration, volunteers retain their voluntary spirit providing they avoid becoming dependent on any money received from their volunteering. Structurally, volunteers may serve formally in collaboration with legally chartered organizations or informally in situations involving small groups, sets, or networks of friends, neighbors, and the like that have no such legal basis. Finally, it follows from what was said previously about altruism and self-interest in volunteering that both the volunteers and those whom they help find benefits in such activity. It should be noted, however, that the field of serious leisure, or *career*, volunteering, even if it does cover considerable ground, is still narrower than that of volunteering in general, which includes helping as casual leisure and volunteering in projects as project-based leisure.

The descriptive taxonomy published by the author (Stebbins, 1998a, pp. 74-80), which consists of sixteen types of organizational volunteering, shows the scope of career volunteering. Career volunteers provide a great variety of services in education, science, civic affairs (advocacy projects, professional and labor organizations), spiritual development, health, economic development, religion, politics, government (programs and services), human relationships, recreation, and the arts. Some of these volunteers work in the fields of safety or the physical environment, whereas others prefer to provide necessities (e.g., food, clothing, shelter) or support services. Although much of career volunteering appears to be connected in some way with an organization of some sort, the scope of this leisure can be even broader, including the kinds of helping devoted individuals do for social movements or for neighbors or friends. Still, the definition of serious leisure restricts attention everywhere to volunteering in which the participant finds a career in acquiring a combination of skill, knowledge, and experience gained through more or less continuous and substantial helping. Therefore, one-time donations of money, organs, services, and so forth are more accurately classified as voluntary action of another sort, as are instances of casual volunteering, which include ushering, stuffing envelops, and handing out programs as an aid to commercial, professional, or serious leisure undertakings (Stebbins, 1996b).

My own study of francophone volunteers in urban Alberta, Canada (Stebbins, 1998d) concentrated on the careers, costs and rewards, lifestyles, and community contributions of "key" volunteers. A key volunteer is a highly committed organizational or communitarian servant, working in one or two enduring, official, responsible posts within one or more grassroots groups or organizations. One section of the study dealt with two questions, both being sources of considerable confusion in the field of research on voluntary action and citizen participation: is volunteering done by choice or by obligation and is it done as work or as leisure? The study revealed that most of the Alberta key volunteers feel a general obligation to volunteer in their local francophone community, but that they also say they may choose the particular posts they will work in and how long they will stay in there.

Casual leisure volunteering and volunteering in leisure projects will be considered in chapter 3.

Six Distinguishing Qualities

Serious leisure is further defined by six distinguishing qualities (or characteristics, as they are sometimes described), found among amateurs, hobbyists, and volunteers alike (Stebbins, 1992a, pp. 6-8). One is the occasional need to *persevere*, such as in confronting danger (Fine, 1988, p. 181), supporting a team during a losing season (Gibson, Willming, and Holdnak, 2002, pp. 405-408), or managing embarrassment (Floro, 1978, p. 198). Yet, it is clear that positive feelings about the activity come, to some extent, from sticking with it through thick and thin, from conquering adversity. A second quality is, as already indicated, that of finding a leisure *career* in the endeavor, shaped as it is by its own special contingencies, turning points and stages of achievement or involvement. Because of the widespread tendency to see the idea of career as applying only to occupations, note that, in this definition, the term is much more broadly used, following Goffman's (1961, pp. 127-128) elaboration of the concept of "moral career." Broadly conceived of, careers are available in all substantial, complicated roles, including especially those in work, leisure, deviance, politics, religion, and interpersonal relationships.

Careers in serious leisure commonly rest on a third quality: significant personal *effort* using their specially acquired *knowledge, training, experience,* or *skill,* and, indeed at times, all four. Examples include such characteristics as showmanship, athletic prowess, scientific knowledge, and long experience in a role. Fourth, eight *durable benefits,* or broad outcomes, of serious leisure have so far been identified, mostly from research on amateurs. They are self-actualization, self-enrichment, self-expression, regeneration or renewal of self, feelings of accomplishment, enhancement of self-image, social interaction and belongingness, and lasting physical products of the activity (e.g., a painting, scientific paper, piece of furniture). A further benefit—self-gratification, or the combination of superficial enjoyment and deep personal fulfilment—is also one of the main benefits of casual leisure, to the extent that the enjoyable part dominates. In general a benefit is an agreeable outcome, anticipated or not, of a person's participation in a leisure activity. That outcome may be anything appealing to the participant, whether physical, social, psychological, or something else. Durable benefits number among the consequences of pursuing serious leisure, and are therefore not to be confused with its motivational antecedents: the rewards of such activity (discussed later).[1]

A fifth quality of serious leisure is the *unique ethos* that grows up around each instance of it. An ethos is the spirit of the community of serious leisure participants, as manifested in shared attitudes, practices, values, beliefs, goals, and so on. The social world of the participants is the organizational milieu in which the associated ethos—at bottom a cultural formation—is expressed (as attitudes, beliefs, values) or realized (as practices, goals). Unruh (1980, p. 277) developed the following definition of social world:

> A *social world* must be seen as a unit of social organization which is diffuse and amorphous in character. Generally larger than groups or organizations, social worlds are not necessarily defined by formal boundaries, membership lists, or spatial territory....A social world must be seen as an internally recognizable constellation of actors, organizations, events, and practices which have coalesced into a perceived sphere of interest and involvement for participants. Characteristically, a social world lacks a powerful centralized authority structure and is delimited by. . .effective communication and not territory nor formal group membership.

In a second paper Unruh added that the typical social world is characterized by voluntary identification, by a freedom to enter into and depart from it (Unruh, 1979). Moreover, because it is so diffuse, ordinary members are only partly involved in the full range of its activities. After all, a social world may be local, regional, multiregional, national, even, international. Third, people in complex societies such as Canada and the United States are often members of several social worlds. Finally, social worlds are held together, to an important degree, by semiformal, or mediated, communication. They are rarely heavily bureaucratized yet, due to their diffuseness, they are rarely characterized by intense face-to-face interaction. Rather, communication is typically mediated by newsletters, posted notices, telephone messages, mass mailings, Internet communications, radio and television announcements, and similar means, with the strong possibility that the Internet could become the most popular of these in the future.

The sixth quality revolves around the preceding five: participants in serious leisure tend to *identify* strongly with their chosen pursuits. In contrast, casual leisure, though hardly humiliating or despicable, is nonetheless too fleeting, mundane, and commonplace for most people to find a distinctive identity there. In fact, as the next section shows, a serious leisure pursuit can hold greater appeal as an identifier than a person's work role.

Rewards, Costs, and Motivation

In addition, research on serious leisure has led to the discovery of a distinctive set of rewards for each activity examined (Stebbins, 2001a, p. 13). In these studies the participant's leisure fulfilment has been found to stem from a constellation of particular rewards gained from the activity, be it boxing, ice climbing, or giving dance lessons to the elderly.[2] Furthermore, the rewards are not only fulfilling in themselves, but also fulfilling as counterweights to the costs encountered in the activity. That is, every serious leisure activity contains its own combination of tensions, dislikes and disappointments, which each participant must confront in some way. For instance, an amateur football player may not always like attending daily practices, being bested occasionally by more junior players when there, and being required to sit on the sidelines from time to time while others get experience at his position. Yet he may still regard this activity as highly fulfilling—as (serious) leisure—because it also offers certain powerful rewards.

Put more precisely, then, the drive to find fulfillment in serious leisure is the drive to experience the rewards of a given leisure activity, such that its costs are seen by the participant as more or less insignificant by comparison. This is at once the meaning of the activity for the participant and his or her motivation for engaging in it. It is this motivational sense of the concept of reward that distinguishes it from the idea of durable benefit set out earlier, a concept that, as I said, emphasizes outcomes rather than antecedent conditions. Nonetheless, the two ideas constitute two sides of the same social psychological coin.

The rewards of a serious leisure pursuit are the more or less routine values that attract and hold its enthusiasts. Every serious leisure career both frames and is framed by the continuous search for these rewards, a search that takes months, and in many pursuits, years before the participant consistently finds deep fulfillment in his or her amateur, hobbyist, or volunteer role. The ten rewards presented below emerged in the course of various exploratory studies of amateurs, hobbyists, and career volunteers. As the following list shows, the rewards of serious leisure are, numerically speaking, predominantly personal.

Personal rewards

1. Personal enrichment (cherished experiences)
2. Self-actualization (developing skills, abilities, knowledge)
3. Self-expression (expressing skills, abilities, knowledge already developed)
4. Self-image (known to others as a particular kind of serious leisure participant)
5. Self-gratification (combination of superficial enjoyment and deep fulfilment)
6. Re-creation (regeneration) of oneself through serious leisure after a day's work
7. Financial return (from a serious leisure activity)

Social rewards

8. Social attraction (associating with other serious leisure participants, with clients as a volunteer, participating in the social world of the activity)
9. Group accomplishment (group effort in accomplishing a serious leisure project; senses of helping, being needed, being altruistic)
10. Contribution to the maintenance and development of the group (including senses of helping, being needed, being altruistic in making the contribution)

In the various studies on amateurs, hobbyists, and volunteers, these rewards, depending on the activity, were often given different weightings by the interviewees to reflect their importance relative to each other. Nonetheless, some common ground exists, for the studies do show that, in terms of their personal importance, most serious leisure participants rank self-enrichment and self-gratification as number one and number two. Moreover, to find either reward, participants must have acquired sufficient levels of relevant skill, knowledge, and experience and be in a position to use these acquisitions (Stebbins, 1979; 1993c). In other words, self-actualization, which was often ranked third in importance, is also highly rewarding in serious leisure.

Recently several scholars have joined me in arguing that serious leisure experiences also have a negative side that must not be overlooked (Codina, 1999; Harries and Currie, 1998; Siegenthaler and Gonsalez, 1997; Lee, Dattilo, and Howard, 1994). In line with this reasoning, I have always asked my respondents to discuss the costs they face in their serious leisure. But so far, it has been impossible to develop a general list of them, as has been done for rewards, since the costs tend to be highly specific to each serious leisure activity. Thus each activity I have studied to date has been found to have its own constellation of costs, but as the respondents see them, they are invariably and heavily outweighed in importance by the rewards of the activity. In general terms the costs discovered to date may be classified as disappointments, dislikes, or tensions. Nonetheless, all research on serious leisure considered, its costs are not nearly as commonly examined as its rewards, leaving thus a gap in our understanding that must be filled.

The costs of leisure may also be seen as one type of leisure constraint. Leisure constraints, are defined as "factors that limit people's participation in leisure activities, use of services, and satisfaction or enjoyment of current activities" (Scott, 2003, p. 75). Costs certainly dilute the satisfaction or enjoyment participants experience in pursuing certain leisure activities, even if, in their interpretation of them, those participants find such costs, or constraints, overridden by the powerful rewards also found there.

Thrills and Psychological Flow

Thrills are part of this reward system. *Thrills*, or high points, are the sharply exciting events and occasions that stand out in the minds of those who pursue a kind of serious leisure. In general, they tend to be associated with the rewards of self-enrichment and, to a lesser extent, those of self-actualization and self-expression. That is, thrills in serious leisure may be seen as situated manifestations of certain more abstract rewards; they are what participants in some fields seek as concrete expressions of the rewards they find there. They are important, in substantial part, because they motivate the participant to stick with the pursuit in hope of finding similar experiences again and again and because they demonstrate that diligence and commitment may pay off.

Over the years, I have identified a number of thrills that come with the serious leisure activities I studied. These thrills are exceptional instances of the *flow* experience. Thus, although the idea of flow originated with the work of Mihalyi Csikszentmihalyi (1990), and has therefore an intellectual history quite separate from that of serious leisure, it does nevertheless happen, depending on the activity, that it is a key motivational force there. For example I found flow was highly prized in the hobbies of kayaking, mountain/ice climbing, and snowboarding (Stebbins, 2005c). What then is flow?

The intensity with which some participants approach their leisure suggests that, there, they may at times be in psychological flow. Flow, a form of optimal experience, is possibly the most widely discussed and studied generic intrinsic reward in the psychology of work and leisure.[3]

Although many types of work and leisure generate little or no flow for their participants, those that do are found primarily the "devotee occupations" (Stebbins, 2004b) and serious leisure. Still, it appears that each work and leisure activity capable of producing flow does so in terms unique to it. And it follows that each of these activities must be carefully studied to discover the properties of their core that contributes to the distinctive flow experience it offers.

In his theory of optimal experience, Csikszentmihalyi (1990, pp. 3-5, 54) describes and explains the psychological foundation of the many flow activities in work and leisure, as exemplified in chess, dancing, surgery, and rock climbing. Flow is "autotelic" experience, or the sensation that comes with the actual enacting of intrinsically reward-ing activity. Over the years, Csikszentmihalyi (1990, pp. 49-67) has identified and explored eight components of this experience. It is easy to see how this quality of complex core activity, when present, is sufficiently rewarding and, it follows, highly valued to endow it with many of the qualities of serious leisure, thereby rendering the two, at the motivational level, inseparable in several ways. And this even though most people tend to think of work and leisure as vastly different. The eight components are

1. Sense of competence in executing the activity;
2. Requirement of concentration;
3. Clarity of goals of the activity;
4. Immediate feedback from the activity;
5. Sense of deep, focused involvement in the activity;
6. Sense of control in completing the activity;
7. Loss of self-consciousness during the activity;
8. Sense of time is truncated during the activity.

These components are self-evident, except possibly for the first and the sixth. With reference to the first, flow fails to develop when the activity is either too easy or too difficult; to experience flow the participant must feel capable of performing a moderately challenging activity. The sixth component refers to the perceived degree of control the participant has over execution of the activity. This is not a matter of personal competence; rather it is one of degree of maneuverability in the fact of uncontrollable external forces, a condition well illustrated in situations faced by the mountain hobbyists mentioned above, as when the water level suddenly rises on the river or an unpredicted snowstorm results in a whiteout on a mountain snowboard slope.

Flow was found to be a cardinal motivator in mountaineering, kayaking, and snowboarding, even while it is only an occasional state of mind for participants. That is, in any given outing in one of these hobbies, participants only experience flow some of the time. Meanwhile it is not even this central, or even present at all, in some other outdoor hobbies. It does not, for instance, seem to characterize much of mountain scrambling (hiking to mountain peaks, possible when technical equipment is not needed), backpacking, or horseback riding. By contrast, it is certainly a motivational feature in mountain biking as well as cross-country and downhill skiing. Similar patterns of flow show up in the performing fine and entertainment arts, the active hobbies (especially activity participation and sport and games), and certain career volunteering fields such as emergency medical service and volunteer fire fighting.

Is flow experienced in casual and project-based leisure? Certainly there are thrills to be found there as well, as in a roller coaster ride or volunteer ushering at a concert of a symphony orchestra (hearing thrilling passages of the music being played). But components of flow 1, 2, and 6 are found only in serious leisure (and some forms of work), suggesting that, in the serious leisure perspective, flow is truly experienced only in certain kinds of serious leisure.

Costs, Uncontrollability, and Marginality

From the earlier statement about costs and rewards, it is evident why the desire to participate in the core amateur, hobbyist, or volunteer activity can become for some participants some of the time significantly *uncontrollable*. This is because it engenders in its practitioners the desire to engage in the activity beyond the time or the money (if not both) available for it. As a professional violinist once counseled his daughter, "Rachel, never marry an amateur violinist! He will want to play quartets all night" (from Bowen, 1935, p. 93). There seems to be an almost universal desire to upgrade: to own a better set of golf clubs, buy a more powerful telescope, take more dance lessons perhaps from a renowned (and consequently more expensive) professional, and so forth. The same applies to hobbyist and volunteer pursuits.

Chances are therefore good that some serious leisure enthusiasts will be eager to spend more time at and money on the core activity than is likely to be countenanced by certain significant others who also makes demands on that time and money. The latter may soon come to the interpretation that the enthusiast is more enamored of the core leisure activity than of, say, the partner or spouse.[4] Charges of selfishness may, then, not be long off. I found in my research on serious leisure that attractive activity and selfishness are natural partners (Stebbins, 2001a, chap. 4). Whereas some casual leisure and even project-based leisure can also be uncontrollable, the marginality hypothesis (stated below) implies that such a proclivity is generally significantly stronger among serious leisure participants. Selfishness is an ethical question seldom raised in leisure studies.

Uncontrollable or not serious leisure activities, given their intense appeal, can also be viewed as behavioral expressions of the participants' *central life interests* in those activities. In his book by the same title, Robert Dubin (1992) defines this interest as "that portion of a person's total life in which energies are invested in both physical/intellectual activities and in positive emotional states." Sociologically, a central life interest is often associated with a major role in life. And since they can only emerge from positive emotional states, obsessive and compulsive activities can never become central life interests.

Finally, I have argued over the years that amateurs, and sometimes even the activities they pursue, are marginal in society, for amateurs are neither dabblers (casual leisure) nor professionals (see also Stebbins, 1979). Moreover, studies of hobbyists and career volunteers show that they and some of their activities are just as marginal and for many of the same reasons (Stebbins, 1996a; 1998d). Several properties of serious leisure give substance to these observations. One, although seemingly illogical according to common sense, is that serious leisure is characterized empirically by an important degree of positive commitment to a pursuit (Stebbins, 1992a, pp. 51-52). This commitment is measured, among other ways, by the sizeable investments of time and energy in the leisure made by its devotees and participants. Two, serious leisure is pursued with noticeable intentness, with such passion that Erving Goffman (1963, pp. 144-145) once branded amateurs and hobbyists as the "quietly disaffiliated." People with such orientations toward their leisure are marginal compared with people who go in for the ever-popular forms of much of casual leisure.

Career

Leisure career, introduced earlier as a central component of the definition of serious leisure and as one of its six distinguishing qualities, is important enough as a concept in this exposition of the basics of this form of leisure to warrant still further discussion. One reason for this special treatment is that a person's sense of the unfolding of his or her career in any complex role, leisure roles included, can be, at times, a powerful motive to act there.[5] And, in attempting to counter Parker's (1996, pp. 327-328) criticism of my use of the idea of career in the serious leisure perspective, note that I am speaking, here, of "subjective career," as opposed to the "objective" kind (Stebbins, 1970a; 2001a, pp.129-131). For example, a woman who knits a sweater that a friend praises highly is likely to feel some sense of her own abilities in this hobby and be motivated to continue in it, possibly trying more complicated patterns. Athletes who win awards for excellence in their sport can get from this a similar jolt of enthusiasm for participation there.

Exploratory research on careers in serious leisure has so far proceeded from a broad, rather loose definition: a leisure career is the typical course, or passage, of a type of amateur, hobbyist, or volunteer that carries the person into and through a leisure role and possibly into and through a work role. The essence of any career, whether in work, leisure, or elsewhere, lies in the temporal continuity of the activities associated with it. Moreover, we are accustomed to thinking of this continuity as one of accumulating rewards and prestige, as progress along these lines from some starting point, even though continuity may also include career retrogression. In the worlds of sport and entertainment, for instance, athletes and artists may reach performance peaks early on, after which the prestige and rewards diminish as the limelight shifts to younger, sometimes more capable practitioners. Serious leisure careers have been empirically examined in my own research and that of Baldwin and Norris (1999).

Career continuity may occur predominantly within, between, or outside organizations. Careers in organizations such as a community orchestra or hobbyist association only rarely involve the challenge of the "bureaucratic crawl," to use the imagery of C. Wright Mills. In other words, little or no hierarchy exists for them to climb. Nevertheless, the amateur or hobbyist still gains a profound sense of continuity, and hence career, from his or her more or less steady development as a skilled, experienced, and knowledgeable participant in a particular form of serious leisure and from the deepening fulfilment that accompanies this kind of personal growth. Moreover some volunteer careers may be intra-organizational, a good example of this being available in the world of the barbershop singer (Stebbins, 1996a, chap. 3).

Still, many amateurs and volunteers as well as some hobbyists have careers that bridge two or more organizations. For them, career continuity stems from their growing reputations as skilled, knowledgeable practitioners and, based on this image, from finding increasingly better leisure opportunities available through various outlets (as in different teams,

orchestras, organizations, tournaments, exhibitions, journals, conferences, contests, shows, and the like). Meanwhile, still other amateurs and
hobbyists who pursue noncollective lines of leisure (e.g., tennis, painting, clowning, golf, entertainment magic) are free of even this marginal
affiliation with an organization. The extra-organizational career of the
informal volunteer, the forever willing and sometimes highly skilled and
knowledgeable helper of friends and neighbors is of this third type.

Serious leisure participants who stick with their activities eventually
pass through four, possibly five career stages: beginning, development,
establishment, maintenance, and decline. But the boundaries separating
these stages are imprecise, for as the condition of continuity suggests,
the participant passes largely imperceptibly from one to the next. The
beginning lasts as long as is necessary for interest in the activity to take
root. Development begins when the interest has taken root and its pursuit
becomes more or less routine and systematic. Serious leisure participants
advance to the establishment stage once they have moved beyond the
requirement of having to learn the basics of their activity. During the
maintenance stage, the leisure career is in full bloom; here participants
are now able to enjoy to the utmost their pursuit of it, the uncertainties
of getting established having been, for the most part, put behind them.
By no means all serious leisure participants face decline, but those who
do, may experience it because of deteriorating mental or physical skills.
And it appears to happen—though I know not how often—that the bloom
simply falls off the rose; that leisure participants sometimes reach a point
of diminishing returns in the activity, getting out of it all they believe is
available for them. Now it is less fulfilling, perhaps on occasion even
boring. Now it is time to search for a new activity. A more detailed description of the career framework and its five stages, along with empirical
support for them, is available elsewhere (Stebbins, 1992a, chap. 5; on
hobbyist careers, see Stebbins, 1996a; Heuser, 2005).

Although this can vary according to where in their careers participants
in serious leisure are, I have observed over the years that, at any one
point time, they can be classified as either *devotees* or *participants*. The
devotees are highly dedicated to their pursuits, whereas the participants
are only moderately interested in it, albeit significantly more so than
dabblers. Participants typically greatly outnumber devotees. Along this
dimension devotees and participants are operationally distinguished
primarily by the different amounts of time they commit to their hobby,
as manifested in engaging in the core activity, training or preparing for
it, reading about it, and the like.

This is, however, a rather crude scale of intensity of involvement in a serious leisure activity, a weakness not missed by Siegenthaler and O'Dell (2003, p. 51). Their findings from a study of older golfers and successful aging revealed that data on leisure career are more effectively considered according to three types, labeled by them as "social," "moderate," and "core devotee." The moderate is equivalent to the participant, whereas the social player falls into a class of players who are more skilled and involved than dabblers but less skilled and involved than the moderates (participants). To keep terminology consistent with past theory and research and the generality of the earlier two terms, I suggest we calibrate this new, more detailed, involvement scale with appropriate, new terms: *participant, moderate devotee,* and *core devotee.* The important contribution by Siegenthaler and O'Dell to revision of this part of the Perspective is acknowledged.

Recreational Specialization

Recreational specialization and serious leisure have in common that they are complex leisure activity: activity requiring some combination of substantial skill, knowledge, and experience to carry out in a fulfilling way its many different and highly interrelated facets. Recreational specialization is both process and product. As process it refers to a progressive narrowing of interests within a complex leisure activity; 'a continuum of behavior from the general to the particular' (Bryan, 1977, p. 175). As product it refers to the fact that a person has, in this fashion, narrowed his interests in the activity. Hobson Bryan coined the term and pioneered the theoretical perspective in which it is embedded. An inductive, participant observational study of specialization in trout fishing served as the empirical basis for his theoretical ideas. Bryan observed that, as people become more immersed in this hobby, they tend to specialize in it. That is, they come, for instance, to fish only a certain species of trout, fish using only "barbless" hooks, fish only with artificial flies, or fish in either streams or lakes. Thus there is often also a specialization in equipment accompanying this narrowing of interests.

Bryan found a historical sense of growing personal involvement and improvement was seen, in itself, to spur people on in their participation in and commitment to their specialty. Scott and Schafer (2001), after reviewing the literature on recreational specialization, developed their own conceptualization of it, seeing it as a process entailing a progression in behavior, skill, and commitment. That is, with increasing skill, knowledge, and commitment related to a complex leisure activity, behavior tends to become ever more focused on a specialized facet of it, usually accomplished in parallel with a growing emotional attachment to it.

The similarities and differences between serious leisure and recreational specialization are considered in detail in a separate publication (Stebbins, 2005g). In general the easiest way to compare the two is to show where recreational specialization fits within the serious leisure framework. Taken as an aspect of serious leisure, specialization may be seen as part of the leisure career experienced in those complex activities that offer participants who want to focus their interests an opportunity to specialize. In particular, when specialization occurs, it unfolds as a process within the development or establishment stage, possibly spanning the two, or should the participant change specialties, it unfolds within the maintenance stage. In career terminology, developing a specialty is a career turning point.

Conclusions

This, then, is the basic conceptualization of serious leisure. It represents my latest thinking on this form, including my most recent efforts to shape the definitions of key terms. It also includes either reference to or, more profoundly, incorporation of several related ideas that add clarity and depth to this basic statement. Thus constraint, benefit (in the broad sense), and involvement have been referenced here for the first time in the serious leisure perspective. This reference is superficial, and much remains to be done to bring these three into the Perspective as integral concepts. But at least initial mention has now been made of them. The subject has been broached. By comparison I have given here, for the first time, somewhat more attention to recreational specialization; it now plays a more visible role in the serious leisure side of the Perspective. Here too, however, some theoretic work remains to be done.

Some time ago I introduced flow in the discussion of motivation and serious leisure (see chap. 6 for information on when this occurred). Yet, every time I write about flow and serious leisure, I seem to find some more ways of relating the two. As noted flow is not experienced in many kinds of serious leisure, but in those where it is experienced, it is highly valued; it is a powerful reason for engaging in the core activity. So the present statement is quite likely not the last word on flow and serious leisure; the appeal of flow is such that it will continue to be studied, and as a result, theory in this area will continue to grow and change.

So, while research and theorizing continue in the area of flow, work is also being carried out on other aspects of serious leisure. It is to this latest empirical support for this form that we now turn.

Notes

1. This definition of durable benefit is similar, if not identical, to the first of Driver's (2003, p. 31) three definitions of benefit. Driver's work makes it clear that the concept of benefit in leisure studies is far broader than that of durable benefit used in the serious leisure perspective.

2. I have recently taken to using the term "fulfillment," because it points to a fulfilling experience, or more precisely, to a set of chronological experiences leading to development to the fullest of a person's gifts and character, to development of that person's full potential, which is certainly both a reward and a benefit of serious leisure. "Satisfaction," the term I once used, sometimes refers to a satisfying experience that is fun or enjoyable (also referred to as gratifying). In another sense this noun may refer to meeting or satisfying a need or want. In neither instance does satisfaction denote the preferred sense of fulfillment just presented (Stebbins, 2004d).

3. Flow has also been conceptualized in leisure studies as "situational involvement" (see McIntyre, 2003, p. 269).

4. One of my respondents in the baseball study (Stebbins, 1979) actually said as much, though he said he loved his girlfriend more than he loved football (which he did not play). He did not seem to be joking.

5. "Enduring involvement," as examined in the social psychology of leisure, bears a close relationship to the idea of leisure career. For example enduring involvement, unlike situational involvement (see note 3, this chapter), is seen as a continuum. McIntyre (2003) offers a summary of theory and research on this concept.

2

Recent Research on Serious Leisure

Chapter 8 in Stebbins (2001) is a review of empirical and theoretic works bearing on serious leisure that were published prior to approximately 2000. The studies reported there served to support, in varying degrees, several aspects of the Perspective. This chapter, then, bears on material published since that year. In covering it I will follow the order in which the basic Perspective was presented in the preceding chapter. That is the most recent empirical and theoretic works concerning serious leisure in general were presented and integrated in chapter 1 into the basic statement. In the present chapter we will look, more particularly, at works concerned with amateurism, then hobbyist activities, and finally, career volunteering. As in Stebbins (2001), to be considered for this review, each work discussed has to center substantially, if not wholly, on serious leisure or, in a few instances, provide rare ethnographic data on a serious leisure activity. Note, however, that not all recent research on serious leisure is considered in this chapter, for some of it is more appropriately discussed in relation to synthesizing the Perspective (chap. 4) or to extending it (chap. 5).

Amateur Activities

The decision, taken in chapter 1, to abandon the sociological definition of professional in favor of a simpler though more relevant economic definition harmonizes well with many amateur and hobbyist activities of recent origin. Economic professionals work in some of these new fields, which have not, however, been in existence long enough to allow a sociological profession to evolve. Indeed one may never evolve, for such a development is by no means inevitable. Several hobbyist fields (most being the subtypes of activity participation and sports and games) have shown a tendency over the years to remain essentially non-professional, among them scrap booking, ultimate Frisbee, sport hunting, and mountain trekking.

Notwithstanding the theoretic relationship between amateurs, hobbyists, and professionals, rather few studies of the first two have addressed themselves to this issue (exceptions will be discussed in the hobbyist section of this chapter). Failure to do so does not generally invalidate the data collected in this research, but it does leave that research in conceptual limbo. I have always tried to establish the nature of the professional relationship with the amateur group under investigation (e.g., Stebbins, 1993a [magic]; 1982b [astronomy]), and with respect to hobbies, have always striven to determine that no economic profession exists (e.g., Stebbins, 1996a [barbershop]; 2005c [mountain hobbies]). It would be good for theoretic development in the serious leisure perspective were other researchers to follow this lead.

Finally it is interesting to observe that, since the second stocktaking (Stebbins, 2001a), there has been comparatively little work to report on amateurs done in the name of serious leisure, compared with the substantially larger volume of work carried out in this vein on hobbyists and career volunteers. In my view this is as it should be, for the Perspective got its start in the study of amateurs, and the bulk of the early investigations there were on this type of leisure. Research on hobbies and career volunteer fields has now multiplied to fill this gap, however, giving this part of the Perspective a much more even empirical foundation.

Nevertheless Puddephatt's recent work on chess players does extend the tradition of research on amateurs. Although his first publication from this study deals mostly with questions arising out of the field of symbolic interactionism, he does report on the flow these enthusiasts experience while playing in a match (Puddephatt, 2003, pp. 272-278). Referring to it as "engrossment," he notes how players find this state of mind at once exciting and absolutely essential for good chess. For, with engrossment, comes the level of concentration so necessary for winning matches. A later report from the same study centers on, among other considerations, the leisure careers of chess players (Puddephatt, 2005). Here he shows how they advance through a six-stage rating system, starting with beginner and moving on, with growing competence and self-confidence, to weak club player, intermediate club player, expert, master, and finally, grand master.

Puddephatt's research, though he remains silent about the professional side of this field, is still the first to frame chess players in the serious leisure perspective. This is also, so far as I know, the first application of flow theory to chess. Furthermore his study provides some uncommon data on leisure career.

Hobbyist Activities

Most of the new work in the hobbyist field centers on three subtypes: activity participation, sports and games, and the liberal arts hobbies. Bartram (2001) examined the leisure careers of kayakers, as experienced by men and women in this hobby. In studying the five stages of the serious leisure career of her two samples, she learned that, as they participate in this form of leisure, certain contingencies serve to stratify the two sexes. For instance she found that, in this activity, as in others where physical risk is possible, men, compared with women, are more likely to use their bodies aggressively and take risks. From the men's standpoint this makes many females less desirable as kayaking partners than other males. Kane and Zink (2004) also studied the leisure careers of kayakers, noting as a significant turning point, or "marker," development to the level where they could go on an adventure tour and express their acquired kayaking skill, knowledge, and experience. Kane and Zink described their research subjects as "amateurs," who were guided on their tours by professional kayakers working as tour guides.

Stebbins (2005c) also studied risk among kayakers as well as among snowboarders and mountain and ice climbers. Both sexes were found, in general, to put a premium on taking no more than "manageable" risk. Such risk is that felt to be within the range of skill and knowledge of the participant, meeting thereby one of the eight conditions for flow. When risk becomes unmanageable, because of fortuitous conditions or social pressure to go beyond personal ability and knowledge, for example, the sense of flow recedes and so, consequently, does that of leisure. Replacing these sentiments is a significant level of fear, fear of breaking something, of possibly sustaining permanent or long-term injury, of even dying.

All three of these studies provide useful ethnographic data on the leisure careers of kayakers, as one genre of activity participant. Their classification as such is not, however, to suggest that they entirely avoid competition, whereby their activity would become a sport. In fact a minority of Stebbins's respondents did occasionally compete against other people, even while most of the time they competed against nature (i.e., a river or creek). In fact this was the preference of nearly all in the sample. Further, the work of Kane and Zink suggests that kayaking may have professionalized to the point where analyzing it as an amateur activity is at least as valid as analyzing it as a hobby.

Sport, defined as a serious leisure hobby, has continued to generate research interest. Major (2001), using the list of costs and rewards presented in the preceding chapter, has become the first to examine them in competitive running. He found in his sample of twelve male and twelve female runners that sense of accomplishment was a main reward to come from successfully running a race. Health and social affiliation were also cited as important rewards. These rewards and others offset diverse costs, among them, injury, letting oneself down (a sort of disappointment), and for females, fear for personal safety.

Hastings continues with his work on masters swimming, a longitudinal project now over twenty years old. Most recently Hastings and Cable (2005) examined the global diffusion and commodification of this hobbyist sport, demonstrating that the role of commodity agent in serious leisure is by no means limited to the C-PC-AP system described in the previous chapter for bass fishers. Indeed, such an intermediary is a main avenue by which some hobbyists, at first only a handful, gain the status of economic professional in their sport. Obtaining product endorsements and product sponsorships of competitions are two principal turning points marking this change in career.

Even more recently the hobby of bird-watching has been examined from the combined perspectives of serious leisure and recreational specialization. Lee and Scott (2006) surveyed a large sample of members of the American Birding Association in the United States, to learn how these hobbyists balance the costs and rewards of their pastime and, in this regard, what difference leadership in the hobby might make. They developed and tested a model that contains, among other propositions, the one that specialization involves accepting leadership posts that lead to benefits, while also leading to the perception of diminished self-determination. Yet their results show that, with increasing specialization, birders find that the benefits they experience far outweigh this cost and the others that they incur. Lee and Scott's study stands as a rare look at the process of weighing costs and rewards in a serious leisure activity.

Liberal Arts Hobbies

Jones's (2000) research on football fans in Britain provides further support for the validity of the six distinguishing qualities of serious leisure. Additionally he uses exploratory data to build a model explaining how these fans continue in this role when costs seem to outweigh rewards, the principal cost being a losing team. He found that this unhappy situation is made palatable through perseverance and emphasis on one or more

of the following four rewards: in-group favouritism, out-group deroga-
tion, unrealistic optimism, and voice. Unrealistic optimism refers to the
tendency of group members to anticipate that the possible rewards of
belonging to the group will outweigh predicted costs. Voice is the process
wherein fans selectively focus on what they see as positive features of
belonging to the group. Gibson, Willming, and Holdnak (2002) followed
with a similar analysis of American football, in which they supplied
further data supporting the six qualities as well as data supporting the
uncontrollability proposition. They also presented a rich description of
the substantial social world their fans inhabit. Both studies deal with the
liberal arts hobby of sports buff, as distinguished in chapter 1 from the
consumer of sport as casual leisure.

Kennett (2002) provides us with the first study of language learners,
whom she conceptually framed as participants in a liberal arts hobby.
In particular, she interviewed a sample of six intermediate to advanced
Australian speakers of Japanese who were cultural tourists fired by the
goal of further learning that language and its associated culture. This study
gives still more evidence for the six distinguishing qualities in addition
to some ethnographic data about the Australians as cultural tourists.

Other Hobbies

Compared with the other four subtypes of hobby, the making and tinkering pastimes remain understudied. This makes all the more valuable
King's (2001) research on American quilters. In addition to observing the
passion her respondents had for quilting (some said it is "addictive"), she
noted several rewards, including self-expression, re-creation (regeneration), and social attraction. King found in her all-female sample a special
manifestation in quilting of the reward of self-expression: the quilts they
make enable them to express themselves as women through a medium
that many other women understand.

Gillespie, Leffler, and Lerner's (2002) study of people who go in for
"dog sports" may also be classified as a making and tinkering hobby.
That is some dog owners breed and train their pets to compete in various
competitions, including obedience trials, hunt trials, sled dog racing,
and draft pulling. In this sense they "make" their dogs into competitive
animals (see Stebbins, 1994a, for further discussion of this category).
Gillespie et al. found that this kind of serious leisure, like many others,
is often intensely pursued, creating in the process tensions with other
spheres of everyday life such as family, work, and religion. Such tensions
generate the need to continuously negotiate between spheres, so as to

be able to continue pursuing the hobby as well as honoring obligations elsewhere. Indeed, this research looked, as only a few studies have, at the costs that come with engaging in this serious leisure activity, these tensions being one category of them.

Drew (1997), in a study of karaoke singers in fourteen bars in Philadelphia, has given us a rare look at some of the conditions that encourage people to move from casual leisure to the early stages of a career in serious leisure. He refers to his interviewees as "amateurs," though without evidence of even a rudimentary professional counterpart, I will discuss the serious leisure aspect of his study as a kind of hobbyist activity participation (karaoke singing resembles, in certain ways, barbershop singing, see Stebbins, 1996a). Drew's investigation contains some valuable insights into how dabblers become more committed to the art of singing, as they learn to conquer stage fright and come to view themselves as singers with a noticeable level of talent and experience. His research shows how participants discover that they can do something more substantial in the core activity than dabble at it.

Volunteering

Although hobbies have received much greater attention since 2000 than previously, it is the field of career volunteering that stands out for its increased volume of scholarship. Within this field, volunteering in sport continues to be one of the more heavily studied areas. Cuskelly, Harrington, and Stebbins (2002/2003) surveyed a sample of Australian volunteer administrators in sport. Some of the respondents could be classified as marginal volunteers—they felt pressure to give time to the sporting organization—whereas others met the criteria for career volunteers (the six distinguishing qualities). Levels of organizational commitment varied over time, but the career volunteers remained noticeably more committed to their serious leisure than their marginal counterparts. This research underscores the importance of examining serious leisure involvement from the perspective of career, in that, over the years, motivation to participate can fluctuate significantly. But some volunteering in sport, because it is done to provide help for a sporting event, is now, given the newly-arrived conceptual statement on project-based leisure, better interpreted in light of that framework (see the two studies reviewed in chap. 3).

Yarnal and Dowler (2002/2003) continue a long-standing, if not sporadic, interest that both nonprofit sector studies and leisure studies share in volunteer firefighters. They studied fire fighters in Pennsylvania, in whom they observed a number of tensions arising from the fact that they are, at once, both amateurs and volunteers. That is there are professional firefighters, and it is their standards by which society judges the work of these amateurs. At the same time these amateurs give altruistically of their time in a way typical of volunteers, doing so in emotionally charged situations where considerable risk may exist. Others who have studied this kind of serious leisure have argued that these enthusiasts are purely volunteers (e.g., Benoit and Perkins, 1997; Thompson, 1997a).

Be that as it may the volunteer label seems to fit best the nonprofessional firefighters. They offer a service, which amateurs do not. And having a professional counterpart is by no means unusual in volunteering. For example Pearce (1993, p. 142), in her study, comments on the discord that sometimes emerged between professionals and volunteers in paid-staff, nonprofit groups, where the two types performed the same core activities. She observed that such tension arises, in part, because the professionals have more legitimacy—that is, they are formally trained—whereas the volunteers have more dedication—that is, they are inspired by altruism. She also found (pp. 143-144) that tension may occur between the two types over the level of expertise itself, as in formal training (professional) vis-à-vis long experience (volunteer). Such friction boils up around the standards Yarnal and Dowler observed in their research. The condition of whether professionals exist in a field of leisure activity appears to be limited to sorting out hobbyists from amateurs.

Museum volunteering has also been receiving significant attention since the last stock taking. Noreen Orr (2003; 2005) examined volunteers serving in six heritage museums in England to determine whether they could be regarded as engaging in serious leisure. Her interviews confirmed this hypothesis. Additionally, her data revealed that the interviewees experienced many of the rewards typically found in serious leisure, particularly, self-gratification, self-actualization, and self-expression. Of the ten rewards self-enrichment was the least important for her respondents. Edwards (2005) looked at volunteers working in arts museums in Australia, where she, too, found them motivated by several of the ten rewards. She also found they were further motivated by a sense of career in their volunteer role. As for some other kinds of volunteers, those in Edwards's sample were somewhat more motivated by self-interest than by altruism. Graham (2004) provides an overview of the literature on museum volunteering, as well as a report on data on such volunteering as leisure as pursued in museums in Scotland. She found that, for some participants, heritage volunteering offers the distinctive rewards of developing new knowledge and conserving that knowledge and, more broadly, local heritage.

Whatever the type of career volunteering, be it sport, museum, or something else, the question of whether such activity is leisure or something else is, it appears, difficult to answer when posed to volunteers themselves. Stebbins (2001c) asked such a question of a sample of Canadian volunteers, who responded in equal numbers that what they did was work, leisure, or neither of these two (i.e., a third category). On a theoretic plane we have an answer for this question, but I find that, among practicing volunteers themselves, it is seldom raised and, when raised, tends to generate confusion.

Social Capital and Civil Labor

Whereas volunteering has been identified as a pillar of social capital as generated through civil labor, the proposition that the volunteering in question is primarily career volunteering, and hence leisure, has been recognized much more slowly and by many fewer thinkers. Rojek (2002, p. 25) has put the case most bluntly: "Serious leisure adds to social capital through the voluntary, informal supply of caring, helping, and educative functions for the community." He goes on to observe that in analyses of the postwork society, as conducted for example by Beck and Giddens, "the notion of the leisure society is given short shrift" (p. 30). A year earlier I registered a similar complaint about the works of Rifkin and Aronowitz and DiFazio (Stebbins, 2001a, pp. 149-152).

Moreover this point has still not sunk in. For instance volunteering is as close as Halpern (2005) comes in his otherwise excellent overview of the research and thought on social capital to addressing himself to what I hold to be a critical missing link in his chain of reasoning about how social capital is generated. That link is leisure, and it is in leisure that true volunteer activities are undertaken. Volunteering is leisure activity, and so having considered leisure, Halpern is partly exonerated from this charge, even while he fails to conceptualize the former in these terms. But what about the role played by other kinds of leisure? Social capital also gets a mighty boost when people from various walks of local community life come together in amateur and hobbyist activities, say, to perform in a civic orchestra or play on a football team, meet monthly to discuss making quilts or building model trains. To understand either the rise or the decline of social capital, also requires knowing, among other things, why people engage in such leisure and what organizational arrangements influence their participation in this way. And, by the way, Putnam (2000), in his celebrated book, *Bowling Alone, did* discuss leisure.

With this preamble in mind, it is noteworthy that a handful of studies have directly focused on the question of volunteering as leisure and, simultaneously, viewing it as civil labor and a contribution to social capital. Arai (2000) studied Canadian volunteers engaged in civic planning and how their efforts contributed to citizenship and democratic participation. Her respondents were identified as career volunteers, as people pursuing serious leisure as board members or service volunteers in three different social planning organizations. Burden (2000; 2001), who, as Arai does, treats volunteers as participants in serious leisure, studied the development of social networks of trust as these support personal volunteering. Burden's action research project helped a small sample of female volunteers in community theater in Australia learn about running such an organization, empowering them in the process by developing in them a capacity for self-direction. And in an entirely different field, Perkins and Benoit (2004) list the substantial contributions to local social capital made by volunteer firefighters.

Bramante (2004) describes a training project he mounted in Brazil, which he designed to stimulate civil labor among youth, thereby enabling them to contribute to their country's social capital. Youth were trained to engage in career volunteering, as both a personal and a communitarian benefit. This included instruction on the importance of volunteers in the community, the role of art and sport there, the psychological development of the individual, the volunteer and the media, and the future of volunteering. Bramante's program has demonstrated its capacity to develop in those who participate in it a sense of commitment to volunteering. Serious and casual leisure are central concepts in the program, which was inaugurated in 2001 and continues to this day.

Other Kinds of Volunteering

Cassie and Halpenny (2003) provide qualitative evidence on the motivation of career volunteering in a sample of Canadian nature conservation workers. The motives pertaining to serious leisure included learning about nature and the principles and practices of conservation, development of skills related to their volunteer role, and meeting certain challenges posed by nature. Altruism was also an important attitude motivating these volunteers. In addition they had "fun," although the way the authors describe it, it could easily pass for the complex reward of self-gratification (reward no. 5). Because these volunteers could take up their role with no special skills, knowledge, or training, Cassie and Halpenny classified them as participants in casual leisure. I wish to argue, however, that it would be more accurate, to identify the latter as neophyte career volunteers at the beginning of their serious leisure career in such leisure. The acquisition of skills, knowledge, experience, and so on quickly puts them on the road to personal development, self-fulfillment, and a career in this kind of serious leisure.

Wearing (2004) has pioneered the analysis of "volunteer tourism," a kind of alternative tourism the goal of which is to "provide sustainable alternative travel that can assist in community development, scientific research, or ecological restoration. It could be further added that they should be ideologically sound travel experiences that contribute to the natural, economic, social, and cultural environments" (pp. 217-218). Wearing argues that volunteer tourism is a subtype of career volunteering, which enables understanding and elaboration of its potential benefits not found in purely economic analyses. That is it is sustainable because its impact is minimal, because it is typically small in scale while requiring little specialized infrastructure. Therefore it thus causes little damage to the environment on which ecotourism and other forms of tourism depend. At the same time, as serious leisure, it contributes mightily to personal development (Wearing, 2001).

Mixed Serious Leisure

The idea of *mixed serious leisure* was first considered in Stebbins (2001a, pp. 126-127), which was done, however, without formal definition. Let us now define it as involvement in two or more types or subtypes of serious leisure that, together, constitute for the participant an integrated pursuit of a more encompassing free-time activity than either of the two pursued alone. Examples are abundant: the violinist in the civic orchestra (amateur artist) who is also president of the organization (volunteer), the variable star observer (amateur scientist) who also goes in for astral photography (amateur artist), and the entertainment magician (amateur entertainer) who also reads voraciously on the history of magic (liberal arts hobbyist). Apart from these categorizations, pursuit of mixed serious leisure also falls, it is clear, in the domain of leisure lifestyle, possibly one that is "optimal" (see chap. 4).

Mixed serious leisure is especially evident in the field of historical reenactment, on which I have already identified some research (Stebbins, 2001a, p. 127). Since then Hunt (2004) has added to this literature through his study of selected activities of the American Civil War Society (ACWS), which he treated as a hobby and type of serious leisure. Much of the research on reenactment fails to regard "living history" as a leisure pursuit, so questions of who joins such groups and why they do this have remained largely unanswered. Hunt's study of a sample of ACWS members in Britain, guided as it was by the serious leisure framework, revealed that they see their activities here as leisure.

Harrington, Cuskelly, and Auld (2000) studied the "hybrid" role of the volunteer/amateur in Australian motorsport. Thus, the same person could be a flag marshal or timekeeper (volunteer) and when he or she was not filling this role, compete in races as member of a pit crew or as a driver (amateur). The authors also analyzed the omnipresent commodity agent in motorsport, placing this person in the social world of the volunteer and amateur there. These agents purvey automotive supplies and racing equipment, doing so through highly visible sales and promotional strategies. Similar commodity-intensive social worlds are evident in alpine skiing, figure skating, major team sports, and as we saw in chapter 1, bass fishing and masters swimming.

Conclusions

According to a rough count of published theory and research on serious leisure, this literature has increased by approximately 60 percent in approximately half the time, the comparison periods being 2000 through 2005 vis-à-vis 1991 through 1999. This count excludes my publications printed during both reporting periods. This proliferation of work in the area is one of the justifications for this book: a stocktaking had become necessary.

We should expect exploratory research to continue on serious leisure, since many established activities have yet to be examined while new activities are appearing with remarkable frequency. But the time has also come for detailed confirmatory work in areas of the Perspective where a solid foundation of formal grounded theory has now been built. One such area is the set of six distinguishing qualities. This review and the one reported in Stebbins (2001a) indicate that most researchers in serious leisure have shown admirable caution against simply declaring a heretofore unexplored leisure activity as being of the serious variety. Rather they have made an effort to empirically demonstrate the presence of all or a majority of the six qualities.

To do this, takes considerable time and effort, the hallmark of the qualitative field studies that are typically mounted under these exploratory conditions. Moreover the data collected in such research are only generalizable to the leisure activity being examined. The need for a measurement scale that will do this more efficiently has been apparent to many scholars in this field for many years. (It is at least ten years ago since I received the first inquiry asking about whether someone has constructed such a scale.) Fortunately, shortly after the publication of this book, a serious leisure scale measuring the six distinguishing qualities will become available for use by qualified researchers.

James Gould is the principal author of this scale, which he has named the "Serious Leisure Inventory and Measure," or SLIM. The seventy-two-item scale—this is its long form (there is also a 54-item short form)—and its development are described in Gould, Moore, and Stebbins (in press). It is the product of Gould's doctoral thesis research conducted at Clemson University. He used a q-sort, an expert panel (e.g., I was frequently consulted on the validity of his proposed measures of various serious leisure concepts), and confirmatory factor analysis to develop the scale, which he subsequently demonstrated to have acceptable fit, reliability, and equivalence across several different samples.

I have tried to stir interest in developing a companion scale to measure the ten rewards, but so far, to my knowledge, without success. It is possible to ask respondents to rank the rewards they say they experience in their serious leisure activities, producing thereby an ordinal scale peculiar to each person. This I have done with every kind of serious leisure I have explored, and have been able to construct a summative ranking of rewards for entire samples of participants. Still, I believe a generalized scale of the rewards could be constructed, which could be administered on a survey basis to study motivation to pursue serious leisure in large populations. SLIM could be used beforehand to separate participants in serious leisure from those in casual leisure and then identify the activities in which the first are involved. A properly constructed scale of rewards would also enable us to measure quantitatively self-fulfillment, a state of mind that was said earlier to stem from a constellation of particular rewards that people gain from their serious leisure activities.

In short, the serious leisure part of the Perspective is no longer strictly exploratory in methodological approach. In fact, several studies reviewed in this chapter were quantitative—some even being analyzed with inferential statistics—thereby adding to the basic Perspective, in all instances, both precision and detail. Little of this has been truly confirmatory, however, in that hypotheses were seldom explicitly stated and tested. Still such testing will undoubtedly come in time.

With the theory and research on serious leisure now set out, time has come to examine the other two forms that make up the Perspective.

3

Casual and Project-Based Leisure:
The Basics

I have no doubt that, some day, these two forms will be treated of in separate chapters, much as we have done with serious leisure. But for reasons that will become apparent in this chapter and chapter 6, casual and project-based leisure, as conceptual frameworks, developed more recently. More precisely, casual leisure, as a concept, is as old as serious leisure, but I only began in the late 1990s giving concerted scholarly attention to the first (Stebbins, 1997a; 2001b). And project-based leisure saw the light of day even more recently (Stebbins, 2005a). Furthermore, as this chapter demonstrates, research expressly conducted in the name of these two forms also lags, though both have been extensively studied under other theoretic rubrics. What research there is has, unlike that on serious leisure with its separate chapter, been incorporated into this chapter on the basics of the two forms. And, as with some recent research on serious leisure, some of that on the casual and project-based forms is most appropriately considered in chapter 5. Chapter 6 contains a detailed look at the emergence of the latter two vis-à-vis serious leisure.

Casual Leisure

The term "casual leisure" is as old as its fraternal twin, "serious leisure," for the first came into this world in the same article that contained the initial conceptual statement about the second (Stebbins, 1982a). In that article and a number of later works, to further clarify the meaning of serious leisure, I frequently contrasted it with casual, or unserious, leisure, exemplifying the latter with activities like taking a nap or strolling in the park or, when pursued as diversions, watching television or reading a newspaper. Moreover, I occasionally added to these definitional statements the observation that casual leisure can also be understood as all leisure falling outside the realm of serious leisure. Over the years, other writers, perhaps inspired by my example, have also delineated serious leisure in these two ways.

Thus from 1982 to the present among those researchers who have written on serious leisure, casual leisure has usually been cast in a residual role. I am perhaps the most culpable in this regard, for I have used casual leisure, among other ways, as a foil to illuminate the distinguishing qualities of serious leisure (e.g., Stebbins, 1992a, pp. 6-7) and to describe its enthusiasts by showing how they are much more than mere dabblers, players, or dilettantes, all basically casual leisure participants. Looking back at them now, I can see that these brief, sketchy portrayals of casual leisure have sometimes been painted in depreciatory colors, which become ever more vivid when contrasted with the appreciatory portrayals of serious leisure (e.g., Stebbins, 1996a, 1996b), leisure activity commonly venerated for its work like character.

Nevertheless, the place accorded casual leisure in the larger world of all leisure is, in significant part, a matter of personal perspective; researchers have different views of it and so do the people who participate in it. For the person presently studying or participating in serious leisure, it is the most important activity of the moment, an orientation that temporarily forces casual leisure to the sidelines. Yet, beyond the spheres of research and participation in serious leisure, it is evident that casual leisure is anything but marginal. Thus, far more people participate in it than in serious leisure, and many of the interviewees in my studies of amateurs, hobbyists, and career volunteers pointed out that they also enjoy and therefore value their casual leisure. In other words, casual leisure is an important form of leisure in itself and, for that reason alone, should be conceptually clarified and elaborated. And although such clarification and elaboration will also sharpen our understanding of serious leisure by further differentiating the two, the principal goal of this chapter is to present a theoretical statement centering on casual leisure as a field of its own demarcated by its own distinctive properties.

Types of Casual Leisure

Casual leisure, which in comparison with serious leisure is considerably less substantial and offers no career, was defined in the previous chapter as an immediately, intrinsically rewarding, relatively short-lived pleasurable core activity, requiring little or no special training to enjoy it (Stebbins, 1992a; 1997a, p. 18). Over the years eight types have been identified.

- Play (including dabbling, dilettantism)
- Relaxation (e.g., sitting, napping, strolling)
- Passive entertainment (e.g., through TV, books, recorded music)
- Active entertainment (e.g., games of chance, party games)
- Sociable conversation (e.g. gossip, "idle chatter")
- Sensory stimulation (e.g., sex, eating, drinking, sight seeing)
- Casual volunteering (e.g., handing out leaflets, stuffing envelops)
- Pleasurable aerobic activity

The first six types are more fully discussed in Stebbins (1997a), while casual volunteering is considered further in Stebbins (2003b). The last and newest addition to this typology—pleasurable aerobic activity—refers to physical activities that require effort sufficient to cause marked increase in respiration and heart rate. Here I am referring to "aerobic activity" in the broad sense, to all activity that calls for such effort, which to be sure, includes the routines pursued collectively in (narrowly conceived of) aerobics classes and those pursued individually by way of televised or video-taped programs of aerobics (Stebbins, 2004e). Yet, as with its passive and active cousins in entertainment, pleasurable aerobic activity is, at bottom, casual leisure. That is, to do such activity requires little more than minimal skill, knowledge, or experience. Examples include the game of the Hash House Harriers (a type of treasure hunt held in the outdoors), kickball (described in the *Economist*, 2005a, as a cross between soccer and baseball), and such children's games as hide-and-seek.

It is likely that people pursue the eight types of casual leisure in combinations of two and three at least as often as they pursue them separately. For instance, every type can be relaxing, producing in this fashion play-relaxation, passive entertainment-relaxation, and so on. Various combinations of play and sensory stimulation are also possible, as in experimenting with drug use, sexual activity, and thrill seeking in movement. Additionally, sociable conversation accompanies some sessions of sensory stimulation (e.g., drug use, curiosity seeking, displays of beauty) as well as some sessions of relaxation and active and passive entertainment, although such conversation normally tends to be rather truncated in the latter two.

This brief review of the types of casual leisure reveals that they share at least one central property: all are hedonic. More precisely, all produce a significant level of pure pleasure, or enjoyment, for those participating in them. In broad, colloquial language, casual leisure could serve as the scientific term for the practice of doing what comes naturally. Yet, paradoxically, this leisure is by no means wholly frivolous, for we shall see shortly that some clear benefits come from pursuing it. Moreover, unlike the evanescent hedonic property of casual leisure itself, its benefits are enduring, a property that makes them worthy of extended analysis in their own right.

It follows that terms such as "pleasure" and "enjoyment" are the more appropriate descriptors of the rewards of casual leisure in contrast to terms such as "fulfilment" and "rewardingness," which best describe the rewards gained in serious leisure. At least the serious leisure participants interviewed by the author were inclined to describe their involvements as fulfilling or rewarding rather than pleasurable or enjoyable.[1] Still, overlap exists, for both casual and serious leisure offer the hedonic reward of self-gratification (see reward number 5, chap. 1). The activity is fun to do, even if the fun component is considerably more prominent in casual leisure than in its serious counterpart.

Shinew and Parry (2005) conducted a rare study focused directly on casual leisure, in which the concept and its various types were used to explain, in their research, university drinking and illegal drug consumption. The hedonic character of casual leisure helps us understand use of these substances among those in their sample of 740 university students who indulged in them. More particularly it was through two types of casual leisure—sociable conversation and sensory stimulation (described by the respondents as "fun")—that this kind of leisure was routinely pursued. No differences were observed in these patterns across sex, race, or membership in a fraternity or sorority. Given its concern with illegal drug use, this study also contributes some needed data on deviant leisure, in this instance deviant casual leisure.

Kerr, Fujiyama, and Campano (2002) attempted to study the emotional return from sport experienced in a sample of Japanese tennis players, some of whom were serious leisure participants, some of whom played the game as casual leisure. Their results suggested that casual leisure is "not necessarily more pleasurable" (p. 286) than serious leisure, a finding that supports my most recent revisions to Reward number 5, which states that self-gratification is a combination of superficial enjoyment and deep fulfilment (see chap. 1). These revisions were first published in Stebbins (2001a, p. 13, see also n. 3), and it is highly likely that Kerr and his colleagues would have been unaware of them. Instead they were guided by the earlier version of number 5 as purely superficial enjoyment.

Moreover, my own observations of casual leisure suggest that hedonism, or self-gratification, although it is a principal reward here, must still share the stage with one or two other rewards. Thus any type of casual leisure, like any type of serious leisure, can also help *re-create*, or re-generate, its participants following a lengthy stint of obligatory activity. Furthermore, some forms of casual and serious leisure offer the reward of *social attraction*, the appeal of being with other people while participating in a common activity. Nevertheless, even though some casual and serious leisure participants share certain rewards, research on this question will likely show that these two types experience them in sharply different ways. For example, the social attraction of belonging to a barbershop chorus or a company of actors with all its specialized shoptalk diverges considerably from that of belonging to a group of people playing a party game or taking a boat tour where such talk is highly unlikely to occur.

Benefits

I have so far been able to identify five benefits, or outcomes, of casual leisure. But since this is a preliminary list—my first attempt at making one—it is certainly possible that future research and theorizing could add to it (Stebbins, 2001b).

One lasting benefit of casual leisure is the creativity and discovery it sometimes engenders. Serendipity, "the quintessential form of informal experimentation, accidental discovery, and spontaneous invention" (Stebbins, 2001c), usually underlies these two processes, suggesting that serendipity and casual leisure are at times closely aligned. In casual leisure, as elsewhere, serendipity can lead to highly varied results, including a new understanding of a home gadget or government policy, a sudden realization that a particular plant or bird exists in the neighborhood, or a different way of making artistic sounds on a musical instrument. Such creativity or discovery is unintended, however, and is therefore accidental. Moreover, it is not ordinarily the result of a problem-solving orientation of people taking part in casual leisure, since most of the time at least, they have little interest in trying to solve problems while engaging in this kind of activity. Usually problems for which solutions must be found emerge at work, while meeting nonwork obligations, or during serious leisure.

Another benefit springs from what has recently come to be known as *edutainment*. Nahrstedt (2000) holds that this benefit of casual leisure comes with participating in such mass entertainment as watching films and television programs, listening to popular music, and reading popular books and articles. Theme parks and museums are also considered sources of edutainment. While consuming media or frequenting places of this sort, these participants inadvertently learn something of substance about the social and physical world in which they live. They are, in a word, entertained and educated in the same breath.

Third, casual leisure affords regeneration, or re-creation, possibly even more so than its counterpart, serious leisure, since the latter can sometimes be intense. Of course, many a leisure studies specialist has observed that leisure in general affords relaxation or entertainment, if not both, and that these constitute two of its principal benefits. What is new, then, in the observation just made is that it distinguishes between casual and serious leisure, and more importantly, that it emphasizes the enduring effects of relaxation and entertainment when they help enhance overall equanimity, most notably in the interstices between periods of intense activity. Still, strange as it may seem, this blanket recognition of the importance of relaxation has not, according to Kleiber (2000), led to significant concern with it in research and practice in leisure studies.

A fourth benefit that may flow from participation in casual leisure originates in the development and maintenance of interpersonal relationships. One of its types, the sociable conversation, is particularly fecund in this regard, but other types, when shared, as sometimes happens during sensory stimulation and passive and active entertainment, can also have the same effect. The interpersonal relationships in question are many and varied, and encompass those that form between friends, spouses, and members of families. Such relationships, Hutchinson and Kleiber (2005) note, can foster personal psychological growth by promoting new shared interests and, in the course of this process, new positive appraisals of self.

Well-being is still another benefit that can flow from engaging in casual leisure. Speaking only for the realm of leisure, perhaps the greatest sense of well-being is achieved when a person develops an *optimal leisure lifestyle*. Such a lifestyle is "the deeply satisfying pursuit during free time of one or more substantial, absorbing forms of serious leisure, complemented by a judicious amount of casual leisure" (Stebbins, 2000a). People find optimal leisure lifestyles by partaking of leisure activities that individually and in combination realize human potential and enhance quality of life and well-being. Project-based leisure can also enhance a person's leisure lifestyle. The study of kayakers, snowboarders, and mountain and ice climbers (Stebbins, 2005c) revealed that the vast majority of the three samples used various forms of casual leisure to optimally round out their use of free time. For them their serious leisure was a central life interest, but their casual leisure contributed to overall well-being by allowing for relaxation, regeneration, sociability, entertainment, and other activities less intense than their serious leisure.

Still well-being, as achieved during free time, is more than this, as Hutchinson and Kleiber (2005) have found in a set of studies of some of the benefits of casual leisure. They observed that this kind of leisure can contribute to self-protection, such as by buffering stress and sustaining coping efforts. Casual leisure can also preserve or restore a sense of self. This was sometimes achieved in their samples, when subjects said they rediscovered in casual leisure fundamental personal or familial values or a view of themselves as caring people.

Project-Based Leisure

In the past I have argued that, between them, casual and serious leisure cover the entire leisure domain. For example, I wrote not so long ago that "casual leisure can also be defined residually as all leisure not classifiable as amateur, hobbyist, or career volunteering" (Stebbins, 2001b, p. 305). I now realize, however, that this is false. My ongoing observations of contemporary leisure have revealed a third form (and there may well be others), identified here as "project-based leisure." Although probably less common than casual leisure, and perhaps even less so than serious leisure, it is nonetheless sufficiently prevalent and important for those who pursue it to justify singling it out for special conceptual treatment.

Project-based leisure (Stebbins, 2005a) is a short-term, moderately complicated, either one-shot or occasional, though infrequent, creative undertaking carried out in free time. It requires considerable planning, effort, and sometimes skill or knowledge, but for all that is neither serious leisure nor intended to develop into such. The adjective "occasional" describes, widely spaced, undertakings for such regular occasions as religious festivals, someone's birthday, or a national holiday. The adjective "creative" stresses that the undertaking results in something new or different, showing imagination and perhaps routine skill or knowledge. Though most projects would appear to be continuously pursued until completed, it is conceivable that some might be interrupted for several weeks, months, even years (e.g., a stone wall in the back garden that gets finished only after its builder recovers from an operation on his strained back).

Examples include surprise birthday parties, elaborate preparations for a major holiday, and volunteering for a sporting event or arts festival. Though only a rudimentary social world springs up around the project, it does in its own particular way, bringing together friends, neighbors, or relatives (e.g., through a genealogical project, Christmas celebrations) or drawing the individual participant into an organizational milieu (e.g., through volunteering for a sporting event or a major convention).

Moreover, it appears that, in some instances, project-based leisure springs from a sense of obligation to undertake it. If so, it is nonetheless, as leisure, uncoerced activity, in the sense that the obligation is in fact "agreeable"—the project creator in executing the project anticipates finding fulfillment, obligated to do so or not (for further discussion of this point, see Stebbins, 2000a). And worth exploring in future research, given that some obligations can be pleasant and attractive, is the nature and extent of leisure-like projects carried out within the context of paid employment. Furthermore, this discussion jibes with the additional criterion that the project, to qualify as project-based leisure, must be *seen by the project creator* as fundamentally uncoerced, fulfilling activity. Finally, note that project-based leisure cannot, by definition, refer to projects executed as part of a person's serious leisure, such as mounting a star night as an amateur astronomer or a model train display as a collector.

Though not serious leisure, project-based leisure is enough like it to justify using the serious leisure framework to develop a parallel framework for exploring this neglected class of activities. A main difference is that project-based leisure fails to generate a sense of career. Otherwise, however, there is here need to persevere, some skill or knowledge may be required and, invariably, effort is called for. Also present are recognizable benefits, a special identity, and often a social world of sorts, though it appears, one usually less complicated than those surrounding many serious leisure activities. And perhaps it happens at times that, even if not intended at the moment as participation in a type of serious leisure, the skilled, artistic, or intellectual aspects of the project prove so attractive that the participant decides, after the fact, to make a leisure career of their pursuit as a hobby or an amateur activity.

Project-based leisure is also capable of generating many of the rewards experienced in serious leisure (discussed in detail in chap. 1). And, as in serious leisure so in project-based leisure: these rewards constitute part of the motivational basis for pursuing such highly fulfilling activity.

Furthermore, motivation to undertake a leisure project may have an organizational base, much as do many other forms of leisure (Stebbins, 2002). My observations suggest that small groups, grassroots associations (Smith, 2000), and volunteer organizations (paid-staff groups using volunteer help) are the most common types of organizations in which people undertake project-based leisure.

Motivationally speaking, project-based leisure may be attractive in substantial part because it does not demand long-term commitment, as serious leisure does. Even occasional projects carry with them the sense that the undertaking in question can be terminated at will. Thus project-based leisure is not a central life interest (Dubin, 1992). Rather it is viewed by its creator as fulfilling (as distinguished from enjoyable or hedonic) activity that can be experienced comparatively quickly, though certainly not as quickly as casual leisure.

Project-based leisure fits into leisure lifestyle in its own peculiar way as interstitial activity, like some casual leisure but not like most serious leisure. It can therefore help shape a person's "optimal leisure lifestyle" (Stebbins, 2000b). For instance, it can usually be pursued at times convenient for the participant. It follows that project-based leisure is nicely suited to people who, out of proclivity or extensive non-leisure obligations or both, reject serious leisure and, yet, who also have no appetite for a steady diet of casual leisure. Among the candidates for project-based leisure are people with heavy workloads; homemakers, mothers, and fathers with extensive domestic responsibilities; unemployed individuals who, though looking for work, still have time at the moment for (I suspect, mostly one-shot) project-based leisure; and avid serious leisure enthusiasts who want a temporary change in their leisure lifestyle. Retired people, who often do have time for plenty of leisure, may find project-based leisure attractive at times as a way of adding variety to their leisure lifestyle. Beyond these special categories of participant, project-based leisure offers a form of substantial leisure to all adults, adolescents, and even children looking for something interesting and exciting to do in free time that is neither casual nor serious leisure.

Finally, comparing it with most serious leisure, it is evident that, at most, only a rudimentary social world springs up around the project. Still, the project can in its own particular way bring together friends, neighbors, or relatives (e.g., through a genealogical project), or draw the individual participant into an organizational milieu (e.g., through volunteering for a sporting event). This further suggests that project-based leisure often has, in at least two ways, potential for building community. One, it can bring into contact people who otherwise have no reason to meet, or at least meet frequently. Two, by way of event volunteering and other collective altruistic activity, it can contribute to carrying off community events and projects. Project-based leisure is not, however, civil labor, which must be classified as exclusively serious leisure (Rojek, 2002).

Types of Project-Based Leisure

It was noted in the definition presented earlier that project-based leisure is not all the same. Whereas systematic exploration may reveal others, two types are presently evident: one-shot projects and occasional projects. These are presented next using a classificatory framework for amateur, hobbyist, and volunteer activities that I developed earlier (see Stebbins, 1998d, chaps. 2-4).

One-Shot Projects

In all these projects people generally use the talents and knowledge they have at hand, even though for some projects they may seek certain instructions beforehand, including reading a book or taking a short course. And some projects resembling hobbyist activity participation may require a modicum of preliminary conditioning. Always, the goal is to undertake successfully the one-shot project and nothing more, and sometimes a small amount of background preparation is necessary for this. It is possible that a survey would show that most project-based leisure is hobbyist in character and the next most common, a kind of volunteering. First, the following hobbyist-like projects have so far been identified:

- Making and tinkering:
  - Interlacing, interlocking, and knot-making from kits
  - Other kit assembly projects (e.g., stereo tuner, craft store projects)
  - Do-it-yourself projects done primarily for fulfillment, some of which may even be undertaken with minimal skill and knowledge (e.g., build a rock wall or a fence, finish a room in the basement, plant a special garden). This could turn into an irregular series of such projects, spread over many years, possibly even transforming the participant into a hobbyist.
- Liberal arts:
  - Genealogy (not as ongoing hobby)
  - Tourism: special trip, not as part of an extensive personal tour program, to visit different parts of a region, a continent, or much of the world
  - Activity participation: long back-packing trip, canoe trip; one-shot mountain ascent (e.g., Fuji, Rainier, Kilimanjaro)

One-shot volunteering projects are also common, though possibly somewhat less so than hobbyist-like projects. And less common than either are the amateur-like projects, which seem to concentrate in the sphere of theater.

- Volunteering
  - Volunteer at a convention or conference, whether local, national, or international in scope.

- Volunteer at a sporting competition, whether local, national, or international in scope.
- Volunteer at an arts festival or special exhibition mounted in a museum.
- Volunteer to help restore human life or wildlife after a natural or human-made disaster caused by, for instance, a hurricane, earthquake, oil spill, or industrial accident.
- Entertainment Theater: produce a skit (a form of sketch) or one-shot community pageant; create a puppet show; prepare a home film or a set of videos, slides, or photos; prepare a public talk.

Occasional Projects

The occasional projects seem more likely to originate in or be motivated by agreeable obligation than their one-shot cousins. Examples of occasional projects include the sum of the culinary, decorative, or other creative activities undertaken, for example, at home or at work for a religious occasion or someone's birthday. Likewise, national holidays and similar celebrations sometimes inspire individuals to mount occasional projects consisting of an ensemble of inventive elements.

Unlike one-shot projects occasional projects have the potential to become routinized, which happens when new creative possibilities no longer come to mind as the participant arrives at a fulfilling formula wanting no further modification. North Americans who decorate their homes the same way each Christmas season exemplify this situation. Indeed, it is possible that, over the years, such projects may lose their appeal, but not their necessity, thereby becoming disagreeable obligations that their authors no longer define as leisure.

And, lest it be overlooked, note that one-shot projects also hold the possibility of becoming unpleasant. Thus, the hobbyist genealogist gets overwhelmed with the details of family history and the difficulty of verifying dates. The thought of putting in time and effort doing something once considered leisure but which she now dislikes makes no sense. Likewise, volunteering for a project may turn sour, creating in the volunteer a sense of facing a disagreeable obligation, which must still be honored. This is leisure no more.

Research on Project-Based Leisure

It is hardly surprising that, given the recent date of the basic conceptual statement of project-based leisure (2005), no systematic research yet exists in its name. Of course there are nearly innumerable studies of projects under the headings of arts festivals, sporting events, historical enactments, and the like, which, however, have been examined using other theoretic frameworks (e.g., event analysis, tourism studies, volunteer studies). Not infrequently leisure is part of these investigations, but it is not conceived of conceptually, as we have in this chapter, as project-based.

On occasion casual or serious leisure has been the subject of research in these studies, but in comparison, neither form explains this kind of leisure experience nearly as well as the project-based framework. Twynam, Farrell, and Johnston (2002-2003) offer a case in point, who by the way, cannot be blamed for failing to consider the project-based conception, it having been published well after publication of their study. The authors tried to explain motivation to volunteer at a World Junior Curling Tournament as the pursuit of serious leisure. Still they found the fit imperfect; the sporting event was too short for commitment to develop and a career to unfold, as happens in long-term serious leisure. They observed:

> Stebbins emphasized the commitment, skill development, challenge, accomplishment, and specialist nature of serious leisure that paralleled career and work specialization. These aspects of volunteering [in this sporting event] need to be conceptualized in somewhat of a different manner so that motivation for serious leisure can be fully understood. (Twynam, et al., 2002-2003, pp. 375-376)

What was really needed was recognition that a new form of leisure had to be conceptualized, serious leisure offering only a Procrustean bed for explaining leisure motivation of the sort they were studying.

Gravelle and Larocque's (2005) study of volunteers at the 2001 francophone games in Canada can be reinterpreted in the same manner. These volunteers served at a sporting event, where they "did not perceive their involvement in the Games themselves as a long-term commitment" (p. 50). Nonetheless, they did need to persevere, for they lacked background skills and knowledge prior to becoming involved with this volunteer project. Indeed, 46 percent of the respondents said they volunteered sporadically, suggesting (to me) that a significant part of their volunteering was of the project-based variety.

Green and Chalip (2004), using the career volunteering framework, studied volunteers at the Sydney Olympic Games. From a review of previous work in the area, they derived several hypotheses bearing on commitment to the role of volunteer. In their survey they found, among things, support for the proposition that a volunteer's sense of commitment to the event, once it was over, was a function of that person's satisfaction with his or her experience of the event. They also learned that this sense of commitment at the end of the event is positively related to the benefits they gained, which included prestige, excitement, and opportunities to learn and help as well as social and professional benefits.

The family may turn out to be one of the more fruitful areas to study project-based leisure. Some parents create projects for their children to undertake in the children's free time. Indeed a certain amount of what Shaw and Dawson (2001) call "purposive leisure" appears to be of the project-based variety. They note that family leisure "seen as a form of purposive leisure, is planned, facilitated, and executed by parents in order to achieve particular short- and long-term goals" (Shaw and Dawson, 2001, p. 228). In purposive leisure parents occasionally organize, expressly for the benefit of their children, free-time activities for the whole family. Further, domestic projects await many a householder, running from developing a garden to renovating a bedroom or rumpus room, with each being done as leisure if it is to escape being labelled an unpleasant obligation.

Conclusions: Leisure, Complexity, and Life Course

We have now completed the review of the basics of the three forms that comprise the serious leisure perspective. People are attracted to the types and subtypes of each form, in significant part, because they find irresistible its core activity. Obviously not all people fall in love with every possible core activity or with the same activity; one person's leisure is another's poison. Some people like to box, while others think knitting is a wonderful pastime. And chances are that knitters think boxing a dreadful activity and the boxers regard knitting as strictly for sissies.

The core activities that constitute leisure can be classified as simple or complex, the two concepts finding their place at opposite poles of a continuum. The location of a core activity on this continuum partly explains its appeal. For the most part casual leisure is comprised of a set of simple core activities. Here *homo otiosus* need only turn on the television set, observe the scenery, drink the glass of wine (no oenophile is he), or gossip about someone. Complexity in casual leisure increases slightly when playing a board game using dice, participating in a Hash House Harrier treasure hunt, or serving as a casual volunteer by, say, collecting bottles for the Scouts or making tea and coffee after a religious service. And Harrison's (2001) study of upper-middle-class Canadian (mass) tourists revealed a certain level of complexity in their sensual experience of the touristic sites they visited. For people craving the simple things in life, this is the kind of leisure to head for.

But if complexity is what they want, they must look elsewhere. Leisure projects are necessarily more complex than casual leisure. The types of projects listed earlier in this chapter are, I believe, clear proof of that. Nonetheless, they are not nearly as complex as the core activities around which serious leisure revolves. The accumulated knowledge, skill, training, and experience of, for instance, the amateur trumpet player, hobbyist stamp collector, and volunteer emergency medical worker are vast, and defy full description of how they are applied during execution of the core activity. Of course, neophytes in the serious leisure activities lack these acquisitions, though it is unquestionably their intention to acquire them to a level where they will feel fulfilled.

So the serious leisure perspective embraces all levels of complexity of core activity. As a result this Perspective enables us to study and compare the full range of core activities as they vary from simple to complex and to learn how people, who desire more or less complexity at particular points in life or, alternatively, in their daily or weekly routine, decide to engage in another core activity or set of activities that better suits them. With the serious leisure perspective we can effectively examine how people adapt to life's demands and opportunities, taking on more complex free-time activities at some points in their life course and simpler ones at other points in it. We can see, too, how they try to balance simple and complex core activities, so as to maximize the amount and level of positive experience available to them at any one point in time in their leisure lifestyle.

Analytically speaking, it follows from what was just said that the serious leisure perspective becomes an indispensable concept when examining leisure across the life course. *Life course* is a broader idea than career, linked as the latter is to particular roles. In contrast a person's life course subsumes multiple roles, which evolve, interweave, and are assumed or abandoned across the lifetime of a person (Bush and Simmons, 1981, pp. 155-157). Furthermore, when viewed sociologically, life course also has to do with age-graded roles and generational effects.

With the three leisure forms lodged in the same frame, where they may be viewed individually or in combination, all remain visible even when the analytic spotlight shines momentarily on only one or two of them. And this visibility pertains throughout the life course of individuals, generations, and diverse demographic categories of people (as based, for example, on sex, religion, education, rural-urban residence). For instance, people who go in for rigorous physical sport in middle-age tend to abandon in old age this kind of complex leisure, many taking up simpler forms such as watching television or doing casual reading. Or parents, suddenly faced with an empty nest, may move from the simple leisure they enjoyed while raising their children to leisure having more complexity, which is appealing for its greater potential for fulfilment than their earlier casual leisure.

In using the serious leisure perspective to analyze leisure across the life course as leisure varies in complexity of its core activities according to the interests, needs, and life circumstances of individual actors, it is best that the Perspective be reasonably coherent. Coherence results from careful, logically integration of the concepts that knit together the three forms. Achieving this coherence is the goal of chapter 4, where the three forms are linked to each other using a variety of related concepts leading to a synthesis of the Perspective.

Note

1. The distinction between pleasurable/enjoyable and satisfying/rewarding, although it appears to be valid in the commonsense world of leisure participants, often goes unrecognized in the social psychology of leisure. In this field, enjoyment is regarded as one possible correlate of flow, well-being, or even leisure in general. See, for example, studies by Haworth and Hill (1992) and Haworth and Drucker (1991). Still, Mannell and Kleiber (1997, pp. 185-186) define satisfaction in much the same way as I defined fulfilment in chapter 1. Moreover, they link their conception of satisfaction with rewards and motivation, as I did in that chapter.

4

Synthesizing the Forms

A number of social scientific concepts have emerged over the years that, each in its own way, helps synthesize the three forms, thereby making for a truly integrated, theoretic perspective. In the main this integration, which I refer to as a synthesis, is accomplished by situating the forms, which, at bottom, are experiential (each of the three forms refers to a distinctive kind of experience found in the core activity), in broader social scientific context. That is each concept has its own place in the larger social scientific literature, while also finding a special place in one or more of serious, casual, and project-based leisure. In other words they synthesize the Perspective as much by being differentially manifested within it as they do by occupying certain common ground across two or three of the forms.

Let there be no mistake: these synthesizing concepts are as much a part of the serious leisure perspective as the basic concepts, those fundamental ideas undergirding the basics presented in chapters 1 and 3. For both sets of concepts help explain the three forms, including their similarities, differences, and interrelationships, in addition to serving as guides for research. The following synthesizing concepts and bundles of concepts are considered here, with relevant research noted where it exists: (1) organization (groups, associations, social worlds, etc.); (2) community (family; work; gender; social class; contributions, including civil society, citizen involvement, and social capital; deviance); (3) history; (4) lifestyle (including discretionary time commitment, optimal leisure lifestyle); and (5) culture (commitment, obligation, values, selfishness).

Organization

The chief point to be made in this section is that leisure, whichever its form, is often organized in one or more of several ways. Note that I say "often," for many kinds of leisure also appear to allow for, if not require, solitary participation, volunteering being the chief exception. Thus, one can, in solitude, play the piano or the guitar, collect rocks or seashells, sit and daydream, or assemble a complicated electronic device from a kit. Volunteering, however, is inherently organizational in the broad sense of the word, since by definition, it involves directly or indirectly serving other people, as individuals or in groups. What, then, do I mean by "the broad sense" of the concept of organization?

"Organization" is used here as shorthand for the range of collectivities that add social and psychological structure to leisure life, extending from dyads, triads, small groups, and social networks through larger organizations of various kinds to the broadest formations, notably tribes, social worlds, and social movements. Accordingly, discussion in this section will center primarily on these different types manifested as leisure organizations rather than on the community or societal organization of leisure, as seen in the sweeping communitarian arrangements that make available leisure services and opportunities.

In keeping with the announced procedure of this book, readers wanting a fuller treatment of the organization of leisure should see my book on the matter (Stebbins, 2002). The present book requires only an *aperçu* of the different kinds of organization common in leisure. So some leisure is organized in dyads (e.g., brother and sister organizing a surprise birthday party for a parent, two friends going to the cinema), triads (e.g., three men on a fishing trip, a classical music trio), or small groups (e.g., church basketball team, several friends who routinely hike together, four couples who dine monthly at a restaurant). These three types of organization are found in all three forms of leisure.

The definition of social network that best fits the small amount of work done on this form of organization within the domain of leisure is that of Elizabeth Bott (1957, p. 59). Her definition is simple: a social network is "a set of social relationships for which there is no common boundary." In the strict sense of the word, a network is not a structure, since it has no shared boundaries (boundaries recognized by everyone in the social network) and no commonly recognized hierarchy or central coordinating agency. Nevertheless, interconnections exist between others in the network, in that some members are directly in touch with each other while others are not.

As individuals pursue their leisure interests, they develop networks of contacts (friends and acquaintances) related in one way or another to these interests. As a person develops more such interests, the number of networks grows accordingly, bearing in mind that members of some of these will nevertheless sometimes overlap. For instance, a few members of John's dog breeding network—they might be suppliers, veterinarians, or other breeders—are also members of his golf network—who might be suppliers, course personnel, or other golfers. Knowing people's leisure networks helps explain how they socially organize their leisure time. In this manner, as Blackshaw and Long (1998, p. 246) point out, we learn something new about leisure lifestyle.

In one of the few studies of leisure networks, Stebbins (1976) examined those of amateur classical musicians. One analytic characteristic of social networks is their reachability, which denotes in a person's network the number of intermediaries who must be contacted to reach certain others in it. Reachability is relatively great when few or no intermediaries are needed for this purpose, as opposed to when many are needed. Thus, in a community orchestra, the concertmaster usually has greater reachability than any other instrumentalist in the ensemble, because of responsibilities demanding direct contact with the majority of its members. For example, this person may be simultaneously assistant conductor, chief recruiter, and disciplinarian, all in addition to being the orchestra's subleader. In the field of leisure studies, Stokowski has devoted by far the most attention to social networks (see Stokowski, 1994, for an overview of her contributions to this area).

At the next level of organization—the grassroots association—serious leisure predominates, though some examples can also be found in casual leisure. The very nature of project-based leisure would seem to preclude grassroots associations from developing there. According to Smith (2000, p. 8): "grassroots associations are locally based, significantly autonomous, volunteer-run formal non-profit (i.e., voluntary) groups that manifest substantial voluntary altruism as groups and use the associational form of organization and, thus, have official memberships of volunteers who perform most, and often all, of the work/activity done in and by these nonprofits."

The term formal in this definition refers in fact to a scale of structure and operations that, in an actual association, may be informal, semiformal, or formal. Moreover, the line separating grassroots associations from paid-staff voluntary groups—treated of in the next paragraph as volunteer organizations—is unavoidably fuzzy, distinguishing the two being primarily a matter of gradation. Both types fall under the heading of *voluntary groups*: "nonprofit groups of any type, whether grassroots associations or based on paid staff, and whether local, national, or international in scope" (Smith, 2000, p. ix). Accordingly all the groups listed in the preceding paragraph are also grassroots associations, as are such formal entities as Girl Guide troops, stamp collectors societies, singles clubs, and outlaw bikers organizations.

By comparison, volunteer organizations offer leisure only to career and casual volunteers and to volunteers serving projects. Volunteer organizations are distinguished by their reliance on paid staff, and by the fact that they are established to facilitate work for a cause or provision of a service rather than pursuit of a pastime. They nonetheless depend significantly on volunteer help to reach their goals.

Pearce (1993, p. 15) holds that by far the largest number of volunteers work in these organizations. But some volunteer organizations may be staffed entirely by remunerated employees, volunteers only being involved as unpaid members of their boards of directors. Hospitals and universities are two main examples. Many foundations can be similarly classified. Other volunteer organizations have a more even mix of paid and volunteer personnel; they include Greenpeace, Amnesty International, and the Red Cross. Finally, some have only one or two employees, with all other work being conducted by volunteers. They are, at bottom, grassroots associations that have grown complicated enough to justify hiring someone to help with certain of the group's routine operations.

Leisure service organizations are not voluntary groups, as just defined. Rather, they are collectivities consisting of a paid staff who provide one of more leisure services to a certain clientele. To be sure, these clients are engaging in particular leisure activities, but the organizations providing them are not themselves leisure organizations of the sort considered in this book. Leisure service organizations are established to either make a profit, the goal of many a health spa, amusement park, and bowling center, for example, or in some instances, simply make enough money to continue offering their services. This is the goal of charitable, nonprofit groups like Meals on Wheels, the YMCA and YWCA, and the Elderhostel Programs.

The next two types of organization germane to leisure have either been covered, in the case of social worlds (chap. 1), or in the case of tribes, will be covered later in this chapter. Let me add here that the richest manifestation of social worlds can be observed in serious leisure, and if found at all in casual and project-based leisure, they are by comparison much simpler in composition. That leaves for the present section discussion of social movements.

The first question here is whether participation in a social movement is a leisure activity. The answer is both yes and no, for it depends on the movement in question. Movements abound that gain members through their own volition, suggesting that the members experience no coercion to become involved. Some religious movements serve as examples, as do movements centered on values like physical fitness and healthy eating. Still, the latter two also attract people who feel pressured by outside forces to participate, as when their physician prescribes exercise or weight loss or face an early death. Thus some social movements are composed of enthusiasts who are there for leisure reasons and other people who are compelled to be there (not leisure). Finally, there are movements that seem to find their impetus primarily in people who feel driven to champion a particular cause, such as the celebrated temperance movement of early last century and the vigorous antismoking movement of modern times. A strong sense of obligation fuels their participation. Those who make up the gun control and nuclear disarmament movements seem cut from the same cloth. Whether this is leisure must be determined empirically through interviews with members.

Social movements, be they primarily of the leisure variety, the forced variety, or a combination of the two, have left a prominent mark on modern and postmodern life. A *social movement* is a noninstitutionalized set of networks, small groups, and formal organizations that has coalesced around a significant value, which inspires members to promote or resist change with reference to it. Thus, considered alone, a social movement is a distinctive form of organization, which provides serious and casual leisure for volunteers. Further there are also likely to be leisure projects for volunteers, as they become involved for a limited period of time with a movement through participating in a fund-raising campaign, organizing a major rally, or lobbying for a certain piece of legislation.

Community

Community is a large subject, and by no means all possible aspects of it have been brought to bear on the serious leisure perspective in the name of that framework. There has nevertheless been research or discussion, sometimes both, on family, work, social class, contributions of the three forms to the community, and deviance. We turn first to family.

Family

In much of the discussion that follows "family" is a summative term for spouses, partners, boyfriends, girlfriends, and other members of immediate or locally available extended family. At times, to be sure, such global treatment of the subject will not do, at which point I will be more discriminating.

My research on amateurs routinely covered the relations the respondents had with their families as these bore on their serious leisure (see Stebbins, 1992a, pp. 108-111). The aforementioned concept of uncontrollability was born of these discussions, signaling that family relations may, on occasion, become contentious and testy over such issues as expenditure of time and money on the leisure activity in question. From such conflict talk of divorce sometimes arose, which was sometimes followed by dissolution, the serious leisure of the respondent being cited as a primary cause of it.

But the same research on amateurs suggests that serious leisure may also have a favorable effect on family life. For example it can contribute to stronger bonds between two or more people when all share an interest in the activity ("a family that plays together stays together"). The serious leisure of one member may become a rallying point for other members, as in the parent or spouse who supports (presumably as an agreeable obligation) the amateur, hobbyist, or volunteer involvements of the participant. And the sense of well-being generated by most serious leisure can favorably affect the family, in that the participant is, as a result, content, high-spirited, and possibly more accepting of others in the household.

There no equivalent research on family in casual or project-based leisure, that is research done under the rubric of these two forms. It is likely that much of what have been observed for serious leisure could also be observed for these two, albeit differently expressed. Thus a husband can, in the eyes of his wife, spend too much time before the television set or at the neighborhood pub, provoking thereby frequent marital spats. By contrast both could enjoy time spent together at the cinema, going out for dinner, or taking a walk. In general casual leisure is less regimented, less bound by schedules and rules, than its serious counterpart, leaving fewer grounds for family conflict in this area. But the relationship of family and casual leisure is vastly understudied, so little can be said here that is not speculative.

It is likewise with project-based leisure; no research exists yet linking it to family. There is reason to expect differences, however, for its limited duration could well keep conflict to a minimum. Family members could well reason that it is better not to contest a member's involvement in a project that is due to end soon, especially if that person finds it fulfilling.

And the possibility exists that other members might participate in the same project, giving all concerned a shared, appealing, leisure interest. Or the project might benefit one or more other members of the family, as might a new sweater, stone wall, or developed basement.

Work

My research on amateurs also routinely covered the relations the respondents had with their jobs as these relations bore on their serious leisure (see Stebbins, 1992a, pp. 111-114). Conflict here has been found to be infrequent, though serious leisure participants of all types try to avoid work that could create major tension with their free-time passion. This was especially evident in the study of the three mountain hobbies, where many of the respondents not only sought work that had flexible hours but also pointed out how much more exciting and interesting their hobby was compared with their job (Stebbins, 2005c, pp. 108-111). Still we may say for serious leisure, in general, that work comes first in any showdown between the two.

Looking at participation in serious leisure from a managerial stand-point, McQuarrie (1999; 2000), in a unique set of studies in this area, examined the issue of organizational support for employee commitments associated with such free-time activity (e.g., time off to present a noon-hour play, travel to a distant city to run a marathon). Her results show that the amount and type of organizational support for such employee commitments vary widely. Moreover she found positive organizational support for serious leisure to have a positive influence on the job-related attitudes of employees. She discovered, further, that supervisors and co-workers differed in their level of support for such leisure, with the latter being more encouraging than the former.

As with the family we lack research specifically focused on the relationship of work and casual leisure as well as work and project-based leisure. It is hard to imagine employers being as generous as the ones McQuarrie studied, were their employees to ask for time off to, for instance, sleep in during a work morning, spend an afternoon at the beach, or even take in the local community fair. But, from the point of view of the typical employee, casual leisure may well look better than the job he or she must hold to maintain personal economic existence. Beauschesne (2005) reports data from a Workopolis poll indicating that nearly one in five Canadian employees dread going to work, while another three in five feel their employment is merely a job, a significantly disagreeable obligation. Belbin's (2003) set of interviews with working-age women who had left the workforce, considered with the Workopolis data, suggest that leisure, when juxtaposed with most work, seems for many people to be the more appealing of the two. For most of these people this leisure is of the casual variety, since serious leisure is not estimated to be widespread (Stebbins, 1992a, pp. 125-126).[1] Project-based leisure is possibly more sympathetically viewed, providing however, that it is one-shot volunteering or other activity having obvious benefit for the local community.

Turning now to another link between leisure and work, note that all three forms of leisure may be experienced as *employment-based volunteering*: volunteering done at the request of the volunteer's employer. Such activity, Thompson (1997b) observes, may amount to an agreeable assignment for the volunteer (experienced as leisure) or a disagreeable one (experienced as disagreeable obligation). What are variously known as "corporate," or "employee," "volunteer programs" are designed to enable and encourage employees in a work organization to serve as volunteers, whether of the career, casual, or project-based kind.

Finally, work organizations may foster other kinds of extracurricular leisure, some of it serious, some of it casual. Serious leisure is offered when a company holds an intra-organizational golf tournament or arranges for an outing of fishing at a remote camp. By contrast the company picnic or annual Christmas party and dinner, is classifiable as casual leisure.

Gender

The matter of the gendered nature of serious leisure was examined in the preceding stock-taking (Stebbins, 2001a, pp. 158-159), which included a review of research to that date. Exploration in serious leisure has continued since. Bartram (2001) found that female kayakers were sometimes rejected by males as partners on kayaking trips on grounds that the former are insufficiently aggressive and tolerant of risk and injury to provide rescue should such be required. King's (2001) study of quilters centered on an essentially female hobby, the products of which express the "women's voice." Major (2001) found that male and female runners were distinguished, among other ways, by a fear for personal safety felt exclusively by the latter.

When research gets more systematically underway on casual and project-based leisure, we should expect gender differences to sometimes be evident here as well. Consider, as an example, *party shopping*. In an event that is almost exclusively female, a woman organizes in her own home a shopping party the centerpiece of which is a set of products she hopes to sell to invited guests and their interested friends and relatives. In the casual leisure (sociable conversation/sensory stimulation subtypes) atmosphere of such gatherings, some food and drink is served as those present talk socially among themselves, while examining and sometimes seeing demonstrations of commodities they may want to buy. The organizer gets a prearranged share of the profit from such sales, with the remainder going to the manufacturer and wholesaler of the products vended. It is possible that Tupperware (house wares) started, perhaps as far back as fifty years, the party shopping trend, which is now emulated by Shaklee (health care products), Pampered Chef (kitchen ware), Fifth Avenue Jewelry (jewelry), among several others (Stebbins, 2006a). In rare look at party shopping as leisure, Storr (2003) studied Ann Summers Parties (lingerie and sex toys) in Britain. Leslie Bella's (1992) research on the "Christmas imperative" (the cooking, baking, buying gifts, and decorating of the home for Christmas done by the mother/wife of the household) sometimes exemplifies occasional project-based leisure. But Bella also found an unsettling problem: a number of the Canadian women she interviewed came, over the years, to think of this project as disagreeable obligation, as drudgery.

Although gender differences will not always be found in studies of serious, casual, and project-based leisure (e.g., Shinew and Parry, 2005), it is wise, when conducting exploratory research on these three forms, to treat gender as a "sensitizing concept." This is Blumer's (1969) term for basic social science ideas that help guide open-ended inquiry, leading thereby to new data on the subject in question. By asking ourselves if there are important gender issues in the activity we are exploring, we will avoid overlooking them when they are, in fact, there.

Social Class

The issue of social class and serious leisure was addressed earlier (Stebbins, 2001a, p. 112), where is it was noted that a great deal of such leisure, at least that studied so far, has been of, broadly put, middle-class participants. There (p. 106) I also noted that we should be on the lookout for serious leisure activities, where the working/middle-class ratio may be nearly 50:50 or possibly reversed. It may turn out that the predominantly working-class activities are mainly hobbies, among the possibilities being pool, snowmobiling, snowboarding, dirt-bike racing, motor sports, and the martial arts. Other hobbies like darts, hunting, and fishing may be found upon examination to attract a reasonably even mix of middle- and working-class enthusiasts. The snowboarders Stebbins (2005, p. 112) interviewed can be described, using as measures levels of education and occupation, as working-class. Still, they were also a young group (average age: twenty-four), suggesting that some of them might eventually achieve middle-class status. Harrington, Cuskelly, and Auld (2000, p. 432) found that those associated with motorsport in Australia, including the volunteers they studied, were generally working class. Adorjánÿ and Lovejoy (2003), using the novels of Australian writer Robert G. Barrett and arguing in contrast to the element of purpose in serious leisure, found that his principal characters indulged in a variety of casual leisure activities salted with the attitude of working-class resistance to middle-class values.

Class is not an issue when it comes to casual leisure, in the broad sense that all classes appear to engage in some form of it. Of course, such factors as money, time, and taste undoubtedly separate who goes in for what, so that class patterns could be determined should researchers investigating casual leisure as such care to do this. The same may be said for project-based leisure. It is, in principle, classless, but the different classes would seem to go in for different expressions of it (e.g., building a stone wall [working class] vis-à-vis taking a special, one-shot, expensive trip to a remote region of the world [upper-middle-class]).

In sum, serious leisure is the only one of the three forms that may have a built-in class bias, skewing overall participation toward the more moneyed and educated groups. Parker (1996) argues that, at least in part, this pattern can be traced to finding a leisure career there, career being, he says, a middle-class idea. But much research remains to be done on this question, for not all serious leisure is expensive (e.g., reading hobbies, collecting natural objects [e.g., leaves, rocks], much of volunteering) and therefore out of reach for low-income people. In fact it may be, more than anything, a matter of leisure education (see chap. 5), of informing all people in all classes about the serious leisure perspective and what is in it for them.

Also at issue here is whether people of all classes can find a *leisure* career in a serious leisure activity. The idea of a *work* career may be foreign to some working-class folks (as Parker argues), but leisure careers for them are quite another matter. As observed in chapter 1, they are based on the person's sense of acquisition of skill, knowledge, and so forth in a core leisure activity. So far as we know, these acquisitions are available to anyone, regardless of class, acknowledging the constraints, stated above, that some kinds of serious leisure do require sufficient time and money to pursue it.

Contributions to the Community

Much of what I have written in the past under this heading has borne on contributions serious leisure participants make to culturally enriching their local community. Thus the local civic orchestra provides classical music to it or the local astronomy club may offer an annual "star night" for public observation of the heavens using the telescopes of members. And local model railroaders sometimes mount for popular consumption exhibitions of the fruits of their hobby.

A broader contribution to the community (and sometimes even the larger society) comes from pursuing serious leisure activities as well as becoming involved in some project-based leisure. This contribution is known as "community involvement" or "civil labor." Community involvement is local voluntary action, where members of a local community participate together in nonprofit groups or other community activities. Often the goal here is to improve community life (Smith, Stebbins, and Dover, 2006). Civil labor, which is synonymous with community involvement, differs only in its emphasis on human activity that is devoted to unpaid renewal and expansion of social capital (Rojek, 2002, p. 21). Beck (2000, p.125) says that civil labor comprises housework, family work, club work, and volunteer work. This is an extremely broad conception, however, which encompasses the wide field of unpaid work, or unpaid obligation.

Rojek (2002, pp. 26-27) argues that, for the most part, civil labor is the community contribution that amateurs, hobbyists, and career volunteers make when they pursue their serious leisure. Civil labor, however conceived of, generates social capital, defined here as the connections among individuals manifested in social networks, trustworthiness, acts motivated by the norm of reciprocity, and the like that develop in a community or larger society (Putnam, 2000, p. 19). The term is an analogy to the concepts of human capital and physical capital (e.g., natural resources, financial resources); it emphasizes that human groups of all kinds also benefit from and advance their interests according to the salutary interconnections of their members.

With one exception casual leisure appears not to make this kind of contribution to community. True, people are sometimes joined in such leisure with strangers, especially these days, over the Internet. This also happens with *tribes*: fragmented groupings left over from the preceding era of mass consumption, groupings recognized today by their unique tastes, lifestyles, and form of social organization. Maffesoli (1996) identifies and describes this postmodern phenomenon, which spans national borders. In this regard, he observes that mass culture has disintegrated, leaving in its wake a diversity of tribes, including the followers of heavy metal music and those youth who participate in raves. Tribes are special leisure organizations, special ways of organizing the pursuit of particular kinds of casual leisure. Tribes are also found in serious leisure, but not, however, in project-based leisure (see Stebbins, 2002, pp. 69-71). Tribes, social worlds, casual leisure, and serious leisure are related in figure 4.1.

Figure 4.1
Structural Complexity: From Tribes to Social Worlds

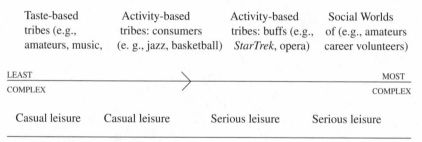

Taste-based tribes (e.g., amateurs, music,	Activity-based tribes: consumers (e. g., jazz, basketball)	Activity-based tribes: buffs (e.g., *StarTrek*, opera)	Social Worlds of (e.g., amateurs career volunteers)
LEAST COMPLEX	>		MOST COMPLEX
Casual leisure	Casual leisure	Serious leisure	Serious leisure

From: R.A. Stebbins, *The organizational basis of leisure participation: A motivation exploration*. State College, PA: Venture, p. 70.

But no contribution is made to the community in the casual leisure just mentioned. Hence it cannot be qualified as civil labor. The glaring exception here is, of course, casual volunteering; it is done expressly for this reason. And, in the course of doing it, volunteers may well meet and serve with people never before encountered. This, too, is civil labor. So we can conclude that such labor is not limited to serious leisure and volunteer project-based leisure, but also finds its place in one type of casual leisure.

As for project-based leisure it may, in at least two ways, have potential for building community. One, it can bring into contact people who otherwise have no reason to meet, or at least meet frequently. Two, by way of event volunteering and other collective altruistic activity, it can contribute to carrying off community events and projects. In other words some project-based leisure (mostly one-shot volunteer projects, it appears) can also be conceived of as civil labor, as just defined, suggesting that such activity is not strictly limited to serious leisure. In fact the mountain hobbyists studied by the author (Stebbins, 2005c) occasionally rounded out their leisure lifestyles by undertaking or participating in (typically volunteer) projects of this kind.

Deviance

Chris Rojek (1997, pp. 392-393) has been virtually alone in his critique of leisure studies as having, in general, "turned a blind eye" to deviant leisure. He noted that, if scholars in this field want to know about this kind of leisure, they must, for published material, turn to the study of crime and deviance. Nevertheless, studying deviant leisure is extremely important for leisure research, for "students of leisure will not only throw light on a shadowy area of leisure activity; they will also contribute to a clearer understanding of how the rules which shape normal leisure practice operate."

Treatments of deviant leisure have now begun to appear (see Stebbins, 1996d, 1997; Rojek, 2000, chap. 4; Cantwell, 2003; special issue of *Leisure/Loisir*, v. 30, no. 1, 2006), and readers interested in it are encouraged to turn to these sources. What is important to note with respect to the serious leisure perspective is that deviant leisure may take either the casual or the serious form (there appears to be no project-based deviant leisure). Casual leisure is probably the more common and widespread of the two.

Casual or serious, deviant leisure mostly fits the description of "tolerable deviance" (exceptions are discussed below). Although its contravention of certain moral norms of a society is held by most of its members to be mildly threatening in most social situations, this form of deviance nevertheless fails to generate any significant or effective communal attempts to control it (Stebbins, 1996d, pp. 3-4). Tolerable deviance undertaken for pleasure—as casual leisure—encompasses a range of deviant sexual activities including cross-dressing, homosexuality, watching sex (e.g., striptease, pornographic films), and swinging and group sex. Heavy drinking and gambling, but not their more seriously regarded cousins alcoholism and compulsive gambling, are also tolerably deviant forms of casual leisure, as are the use of cannabis and the illicit, pleasurable, use of certain prescription drugs. Social nudism has also been analyzed within the tolerable deviance perspective (all these forms are examined in greater detail with accent on their leisure qualities in Stebbins, 1996d, chaps. 3-7, 9).

In the final analysis, deviant casual leisure roots in sensory stimulation and, in particular, the creature pleasures it produces. The majority of people in society tolerate most of these pleasures even if they would never think, or at least not dare, to enjoy themselves in these ways. In addition, they actively scorn a somewhat smaller number of intolerable forms of deviant casual leisure, demanding decisive police control of, for example, incest, vandalism, sexual assault, and what Jack Katz (1988, chap. 2) calls the "sneaky thrills" (certain incidents of theft, burglary, shoplifting, and joyriding).[2] Sneaky thrills, however, are motivated not by the desire for creature pleasure, but rather by the desire for a special kind of excitement, namely, going against the grain of established social life.

Beyond the broad domains of tolerable and intolerable deviant casual leisure lies that of deviant serious leisure, composed primarily of aberrant religion, politics, and science. Deviant religion is manifested in the sects and cults of the typical modern society, while deviant politics is constituted of the radical fringes of its ideological left and right. Deviant science centers on the occult which, according to Truzzi (1972), consists of five types: divination, witchcraft-Satanism, extrasensory perception, Eastern religious thought, and various residual occult phenomena revolving around UFOs, water witching, lake monsters, and the like (for further details, see Stebbins, 1996d, chap. 10). Thus deviant serious leisure, in the main, is pursued as a liberal arts hobby or as activity participation, or in fields like witchcraft and divination, as both.

In whichever form of deviant serious leisure a person participates, he or she will find it necessary to make a significant effort to acquire its special belief system as well as to defend it against attack from mainstream science, religion, or politics. Moreover, here, the person will discover two additional rewards of considerable import: a special personal identity grounded, in part, in the unique genre of self-enrichment that invariably comes with inhabiting any marginal social world.

Youth Deviance

Leisure studies research, such as that of Iso-Ahola and Crowley (1991), shows that boredom in free time is an antecedent of deviant leisure, as when bored youth (the group most commonly examined) seek stimulation in drugs and alcohol or criminal thrills like gang fighting, illegal gambling, and joy riding in stolen cars. The authors were primarily concerned with substance abusers, citing research indicating that these deviants are more likely than non-abusers to seek thrilling and adventurous pursuits, while showing little taste for repetitious and constant experiences. In other words, such youth were looking for leisure that could give them optimal arousal, that was at the same time a regular activity -- not sporadic like bungee jumping or roller coaster riding -- but that did not, however, require long periods of monotonous preparation.

Such preparation is necessary to become, for instance, a good football player or skateboarder.

To the extent that wayward youth have little or no taste for repetitious and constant experiences, then what kind of leisure will alleviate their boredom? Some forms of casual leisure, if accessible for them, can accomplish this, but do so only momentarily. Such leisure is by definition fleeting. As for serious leisure, though all activities do require significant levels of perseverance, not all require repetitious preparation of the kind needed, say, to learn a musical instrument or train for a sport. For example, none of the volunteer activities and liberal arts hobbies calls for such preparation. The same can be said for amateur science, hobbyist collecting, various games, and many activity participation fields. Spelunking, orienteering, and some kinds of sports volunteering exemplify non-repetitive serious leisure that is both exciting and, with the first two, reasonably adventurous.

Yet, the problem here is, rather, more one of lack of known and accessible activities that amount to true leisure, than one of being forced into inactivity or to do something boring (Stebbins, 2003a). Being coerced suggests to the coerced person that no palatable escape from his condition exists. Thus, he must work, since money for necessities will come from nowhere else, or he must give the mugger his money or risk getting shot or beaten. With boring activities, however, palatable alternatives do exist, some of which are deviant, as we have just seen, some of which are not.

Those that are not must nevertheless be brought to light, which is a central goal of leisure education. But what would leisure educators (including leisure counselors and leisure volunteers) teach to chronically bored youth? In general, in keeping with what will be said about leisure education in the next chapter, they should focus not on so much casual leisure but largely on serious and project-based leisure. So this is not the last word on the matter.

History

There is a general history of leisure, of which serious, casual, and project-based leisure are most certainly a part (the standard reference here is Cross, 1990). Of interest in this synthesis of the serious leisure perspective, however, is the history of leisure activities as defined and explained according to one or more of the three forms. In this regard the main point to be made in this section is that, where it is possible to frame an activity in historical perspective, this should be done. The history presented gives another context, another face on the prism, through which to describe, analyze, and thereby understand the activity in question.

Many serious leisure activities have histories, especially the amateur fields, but so do some hobbyist and volunteer fields. Examples of historical framing of research data are available in entertainment magic, Canadian football, stand-up comedy, barbershop singing, volunteering, and selected mountain hobbies (Stebbins, 1993a; 1993c; 1990; 1996a; 1998d; 2005c). Gelber (1999, pp. 11-12) provides a general history of American hobbies, which he briefly acknowledges are serious leisure.

Some casual leisure is amenable to historical framing. For instance a study of contemporary television watching could undoubtedly be enriched by historical data, as could studies of contemporary mass tourism, dining out, social nudism, recreational drug use, and patronization of cinemas. Other casual activities such as napping, window shopping, and informal sociable conversation might be difficult to find or generate historical data on. The same seems to hold for project-based leisure: some types, like volunteering for major events, would be amenable to historical description and analysis, whereas others, like the many personal projects people mount (e.g., a genealogy, rock garden, surprise party) have a chronology of personal decisions and actions, but not a formal history. The very short-term nature of project-based leisure would seem to discourage, if not obviate, historical treatment of much of it.

Lifestyle

A definition of *lifestyle* that fits well in the serious leisure perspective is the following: a distinctive set of shared patterns of tangible behavior that is organized around a set of coherent interests or social conditions or both, that is explained and justified by a set of related values, attitudes, and orientations and that, under certain conditions, becomes the basis for a separate, common social identity for its participants (Stebbins, 1997b; see also Veal, 1993). At bottom leisure lifestyle centers on the ways people allocate their minutes, hours, days, weeks, and so on to free-time pursuits. In leisure studies free time has long been considered a key resource for the individual to manipulate to his or her personal ends.

In other words people taking their leisure make *discretionary time commitments*, which are essentially, noncoerced, allocations of a certain number of minutes, hours, days, or other measure of time that a person devotes, or would like to devote, to carrying out an activity (Stebbins, 2006e). Such commitments are both process and product. That is people either set (process) their own time commitments (products) or willingly accept such commitments (i.e., agreeable obligations) set for them by others. It follows that disagreeable obligations, which are invariably forced on people by others or by circumstances, fail to constitute discretionary time commitments, since the latter, as process, rest on personal agency. In short, this conception of time commitment finds expression in leisure and the agreeable sides of work (which, in effect, are experienced as leisure, see Stebbins 2004b).

Note, however, that we can, and sometimes do, make time commitments to carry out disagreeable activities, whether at work or outside it. Such commitments—call them *coerced time commitments*—are, obviously, not discretionary. Hence they fall beyond the scope of this discussion and, with some interesting exceptions, beyond the scope of leisure (see discussion on leisure costs, chap. 1).

More generally we commonly speak of past, present, and future time commitments (discretionary and coerced) at work, leisure, and in the area of nonwork obligations. The kinds of time commitments people make help shape their work and leisure lifestyles, and constitute part of the patterning of those lifestyles. In the realm of leisure the nature of such commitments varies substantially across its three forms.

Generally speaking serious leisure requires its participants to allocate more time than participants in the other two forms, if for no other reason, than that, of the three, it is pursued over the longest span of time. In addition certain qualities of serious leisure, including especially perseverance, commitment, effort, and career, tend to make amateurs, hobbyists, and volunteers especially cognizant of how they allocate their free time, the amount of that time they use for their serious leisure, and the ways they accomplish this.

There are many examples. Amateur and hobbyist activities based on the development and polishing of physical skills (e.g., learning how to juggle, figure skate, make quilts, play the piano) require the aspiring entertainer, skater, quilter, and so on to commit a fair amount of time on a regular basis, sometimes over several years, to acquiring and polishing necessary skills. And once acquired the skills and related physical conditioning must be maintained through use. Additionally some serious leisure enthusiasts take on (agreeable) obligations (Stebbins, 2000b) that demand their presence at certain places at certain times (e.g., rehearsals, matches, meetings, events). But most important, the core activity, which is the essence of a person's serious leisure, is so attractive that this individual very much wants to set aside sufficient time to engage in it. In other words, serious leisure, as mentioned earlier, often borders on being *uncontrollable*; it engenders in its practitioners a desire to pursue the activity beyond the time or the money (if not both) available for it. So, even though hobbies such as collecting stamps or making furniture usually have few schedules or appointments to meet, they are nonetheless enormously appealing, and as such encourage these collectors and makers to allocate, whenever possible, time for this leisure.

Project-based leisure may be accompanied by similar demands. There are often scheduled meetings or responsibilities, if not both, and though of short range, the condition of uncontrollability can also be a concern. But project-based leisure does not, by definition, involve developing, polishing, and maintaining physical skills, this being one of the key differences in use of discretionary time separating it from serious leisure. Furthermore, with project-based leisure comes a unique sense of time allocation: time use is more or less intense but limited to a known and definite period on the calendar (e.g., when the athletic games are over, when the stone wall is built, when the surprise birthday party has taken place). Indeed one of the attractions of projects for some people is that no long-term commitment of time is foreseen.

Finally casual leisure may, in its own way, generate time commitments, as in the desire to set aside an hour each week to watch a television program or participate as often as possible in a neighborhood coffee klatch. Further some casual leisure, famously watching television, is attractive, in part, because it is often available on a moment's notice—call it "spontaneous discretionary time commitment"; it can fill in gaps between discretionary and coerced time commitments, and in the process, stave off boredom. Additionally casual volunteering commonly has temporal requirements, as in joining for the weekend an environmental clean-up crew, serving on Thanksgiving Day free meals to the poor, and collecting money for a charity by going door-to-door or soliciting on a street corner.

Moreover, in fashioning their leisure lifestyles, people blend and coordinate their participation and allocation of free time in one or more of the three forms. In this regard, some people try to organize their free time in such a way that they approach an "optimal leisure lifestyle" (Stebbins, 2000a). The term, refers to the deeply rewarding and interesting pursuit during free time of one or more substantial, absorbing forms of serious leisure, complemented by judicious amounts of casual leisure or project-based leisure or both. People find optimal leisure lifestyles by partaking of leisure activities that individually and in combination help them realize their human potential, leading thereby to self-fulfilment and enhanced well-being and quality of life.

Culture

I draw here on Alan Tomlinson's (1993) idea of "culture of commitment," my intent being to generalize it to a broader conception of culture in the sphere of leisure. Tomlinson wrote about the commitment "of human actors to the collective forms of everyday cultural life" (p. 9), centering his observations on the creation of cultural products by participants in serious leisure. By generalizing his concept, we may also speak of a culture of obligation, key values, and selfishness, all as related to leisure. They, too, bear on creating the cultural products of serious leisure, and I will argue, those of project-based leisure. Furthermore this is culture that participants both produce and consume, hence most casual leisure, which is only consumptive and not productive, must be excluded from this discussion. As before, the principal exception is casual volunteering.

Commitment

One, although seemingly illogical according to common sense, is the proposition that serious leisure is characterized empirically by an important degree of positive commitment to a pursuit (Stebbins, 1992a, pp. 51-52). This commitment is measured, among other ways, by sizeable investments of time and energy in the leisure made by its devotees and participants. Etheridge and Neapolitan (1985) studied a sample of craft artists in the United States. Their data showed that the amateurs were more serious about craft work than the dabblers, as measured by amount of training and propensity to read craft magazines. Furthermore, the dabblers saw this leisure as recreation, as diversion from their daily routine, whereas the amateurs saw it as something more profound, as an expression of a strong commitment to perfection and artistic creativity. See also the review in chapter 3 of a study of commitment in project-based leisure conducted by Green and Chalip (2004).

Commitment is neither an antecedent nor a concomitant of serious and project-based leisure, but rather one of their most profound consequences. People become committed to a leisure role based on their deep involvement in and attachment to its highly valued core activity. *Homo otiosus* discovers in the course of involvement in the activity just how fulfilling its core tasks can be. Such commitment may also arise in devotee work (Stebbins, 2004b, pp. 17-18), but what distinguishes leisure, especially its serious and project-based forms, is that a related type of commitment may not arise in here, though it may arise at work.

That is, deep involvement in and attachment to a line of activity we have been discussing is known as "value commitment" (Stebbins, 1970b, p. 527); it stems from the many powerful rewards that serious and project-based leisure participants find in their activities. But people may become committed to a role in the sense of feeling trapped in it. They experience "continuance commitment" (Becker, 1960; Kantor, 1968; Stebbins, 1970b). Continuance in a role stresses its penalties, rather than its rewards: it is "the awareness of the impossibility of choosing a different [leisure activity] . . . because of the imminence of social penalties involved in making the switch" (Stebbins, 1970b, p. 527). Sometimes participants want to abandon an activity, possibly because costs of pursuing it (discussed in chap. 1) have become too great, but in attempting to leave the activity, they discover penalties of such magnitude that they feel forced to stay on. The classic example haunts some volunteers, where the president (treasurer, secretary, etc.) of the club or association wants to quit, but no replacement can be found. Of course, at this point, the activity is no longer leisure, and staying on to engage in it, is now a matter of largely unpleasant obligation.

Obligation

"Obligation" is a frequently used but lamentably under-conceptualized idea in leisure studies. Its importance there stems from two facts: leisure activities occasionally or frequently have an obligatory side that some participants nonetheless experience as part of leisure, but that other participant experience as offensive, chiefly because it effectively robs the activities of the quality of leisure choice. To speak of obligation, then, is to speak not about how people are prevented from entering certain leisure activities—the object of much of research on leisure constraints—but about how people fail to define a given activity as leisure or redefine it as other than leisure, as an obligation. In others words obligation is both a state of mind, an attitude—a person feels obligated—and a form of behavior—a person must carry out a particular course of action. But even while obligation is substantially mental and behavioral, it roots, too, in the social and cultural world of the obligated actor. Consequently, we may speak of a culture of obligation.

More precisely *disagreeable obligation* has no place in leisure, since it fails to leave the participant with a pleasant memory or expectation of the activity, a basic feature of leisure (Kaplan, 1960, pp. 22-25). But *agreeable obligation*, an attitude and form of behavior, is very much a part of leisure. It is part of leisure because such obligation may accompany value commitment to an activity and because it *is* associated with pleasant memories and expectations. Still, it might be argued that agreeable obligation in leisure is not really felt as obligation, since the participant wants to do the activity anyway. But my research in serious leisure suggests a more complicated picture. My respondents knew that they were supposed to be at a certain place or do a certain thing and knew that they had to make this a priority in their day-to-day living (an example of allocating discretionary time). They not only wanted to do this, they were also required to do it; other activities and demands could wait. At times, the participant's intimates objected to the way he or she prioritized everyday commitments, and this led to friction, creating costs for the first that somewhat diluted the rewards of the leisure in question. Agreeable obligation is evident in all three forms, though possibly more so in serious and project-based leisure.

Values

It is by way of leisure activities and their core tasks that participants realize a unique combination of, what are for them, strongly held cultural values: success, achievement, freedom of action, individual personality, and activity (being involved in something) (Williams, 2000, p. 146). These values are shared with other participants in the same kind of serious or project-based leisure. Commitment is a consequence of serious and project-based leisure, which in turn, is an outcome of the person's steady and, oftentimes, passionate pursuit of these cultural values.

During casual leisure participants realize fewer of these values. At times specialized consumption by modern youth does lead to individualization of personality, as through participation in one of the tribes discussed earlier in this chapter. Furthermore, choosing a casual leisure activity does evince a certain freedom of action, and the chooser does thereby get involved in something. But, in so doing, this chooser is not, at least while engaged in the chosen casual leisure activity, also realizing the values of success, achievement, and outside the tribal world, individual personality. From the standpoint of the culture of values in the realm of leisure, casual leisure compared with the other two forms, offers the weakest access.

Although I know of no research that actually and directly demonstrates that serious leisure participants believe they have achieved something important and that they are successful, it seems reasonable to conclude that most would feel precisely this way about these two values. After all, compared with others in their reference groups, they have developed considerable knowledge and skill and acquired considerable experience, all of which they have often applied with a certain level of perseverance and creativity or innovation. These two values are not realized through casual leisure, and are realized only in a limited way for many leisure projects (e.g., making and tinkering, entertainment theater).

Serious leisure and to a lesser extent, project-based leisure, help their participants realize the value of individual personality. They are individuated primarily by their exceptional skill, knowledge, and experience as manifested in the core tasks of the leisure using creativity, innovation, perseverance, and so on. Some are further individuated by their social identity as participants in certain prestigious activities (e.g., the well-known arts and sports; celebrated festivals, museums, events).

Selfishness

Selfishness is the act of a self-seeker judged as selfish by the victim of that act (Stebbins, 1981a). When we define an act as selfish, we make an imputation. This imputation is most commonly hurled at perceived self-seekers by their victims, where the self-seekers are felt to demonstrate a concern for their own welfare or advantage at the expense of or in disregard for those victims. The central thread running through the fabric of selfishness is exploitative unfairness—a kind of personal favoritism infecting our everyday affairs.   In comparing the three forms, serious leisure is nearly always much more complicated and enduring and, for this reason, often takes up much more of the participant's time and is much more likely to generate charges of selfishness. For instance some types of serious, and even project-based leisure, can only be pursued according to a rigid schedule (e.g., amateur theatrical rehearsals, volunteer guide work at a zoo), which unlike most casual leisure, allows little room for compromise or manoeuver. Thus imputations of selfishness are considerably more likely to arise with regard to the first two.

Furthermore we can make a similar observation about serious and causal leisure activities that exclude the participant's partner vis-à-vis those that include this person. Logically speaking, it is difficult to complain about someone's selfishness when the would-be complainer also engages in the activity and finds it fulfilling. Furthermore serious leisure, compared with casual leisure, is often more debatable as selfishness, when seen from the standpoints of both the victim and the self-seeker. For serious leisure enthusiasts have at their fingertips as justifications for their actions such venerated ideals as self-enrichment, self-expression, self-actualization, service to others, contribution to group effort, development of a valued personal identity, and the regeneration of oneself after work. Casual volunteering is, however, a partial exception to this observation, in that it, too, can be justified by several of these ideals.

What makes selfishness part of the culture of leisure is my impression—it is generalized from fieldwork, since we lack survey data on the question—that so many participants in all three forms share a tendency to act in this way. Moreover this tendency and the problems it can engender seem to be fully recognized in leisure circles, even if the matter has never been formally studied. Earlier remarks about uncontrollability explain this tendency, and when a participant, seemingly out of control, takes on too much of the activity, imputations of selfishness (whether overtly made or covertly held) from certain significant others is surely just around the corner.

Conclusions: The Role of Leisure Career

Project-based leisure is a distinctive form of leisure pursuit. It is not, as serious leisure is, intended to be an enduring activity lasting well into a person's future. That is, there is no career in project-based leisure constituted of acquiring, over the long haul, substantial skill, knowledge, and experience, as happens when learning to play the violin, working as a mentor with youth, or becoming an amateur rugby player. Moreover, given the short-term nature of the project, it, unlike a serious leisure activity, fails to become a central life interest. And, whereas many projects are embedded in a rudimentary social world, that world is in no way as complicated and evolved as the typical social world in serious leisure. Even the identity issuing from project-based leisure, relatively fleeting as it is, is therefore significantly less anchored in routine community life than its counterpart in serious leisure (e.g., identity of Olympic volunteer as against that of volunteer for Meals on Wheels). But perhaps the most telling difference separating project-based leisure from the serious type is that the former offers a discrete undertaking for people who, for reasons set out previously, do not at that point in their life course want something more lasting, which they would surely get were they to take up the latter.

I mentioned in passing that some people may, as a result of pursuing a leisure project, discover that it, or part of it, is highly fulfilling and that they would therefore like to continue with it as serious leisure. What precipitates such change in orientation? Although this is ultimately a question for research, I suspect that the individual finds in the project hidden talents and aptitudes fanned by a strong desire to develop these in a supportive social milieu that respects them. But that person must also sense that sufficient time and other resources are available for continued pursuit, for realistically expressing a long-term commitment to it. Assuming he or she takes the plunge and launches a serious leisure career, the catalytic project is now reinterpreted by the neophyte as the initial step in that career.

How does project-based leisure relate to casual leisure? As with serious leisure the project-based type is separate from casual leisure. Where casual leisure becomes the precursor of either of the other two, it would appear to occur largely through the practice of dabbling, or dilettantism. Dabbling may, on occasion, inspire a person to try to improve at the activity dabbled in, as when the child who plinks out tunes by ear on the family piano becomes interested in taking lessons on the instrument. With this change in orientation the child, now a neophyte, is embarking on a serious leisure career. The same kind of change could occur in a leisure project, exemplified by the person who uses a camera with minimal skill but decides to seek some formal instruction in photography motivated initially by the aim of creating an impressive photo album of the upcoming high school class reunion. But just how often and under what conditions casual leisure becomes the critical antecedent for either serious or project-based leisure is an empirical question begging investigation.

Notes

1. Polson (2006) estimates that 15 to 25 percent of leisure participants engage in what we call "serious leisure."
2. For papers on serial murder and violence done for "fun," see the special issue of *Leisure/Loisir* mentioned above.

5

Extending the Perspective

In keeping with the language of exploration, the methodological approach on which the basics of the serious leisure perspective rest, research presented in the first four chapters can be said to extend, in two ways, current theory and research in the area. That is, so far, we have extended the Perspective by (1) exploring further previously explored activities or processes, referred to here as *continued exploration* and by (2) exploring, for the first time, an unexplored activity or process, or *initial exploration*. In this chapter we turn to a third way of extending the Perspective, achieved by either seeking new theoretic links or further shaping established ones. This I will label *theoretic elaboration*. The first two are primarily inductive, whereas the third is primarily deductive.

Linking these three avenues of extension, as a common denominator, is the process of concatenation. It was described briefly in chapter 1 as the open-ended approach to research on leisure activities that has guided data collection in serious leisure throughout much of its history. Social scientific exploration leads to grounded, or inductively-generated, theory (Glaser and Strauss, 1967), reached by way of a series of concatenated studies. In social science, "concatenation" refers at once to a longitudinal research process and the resulting set of open-ended field studies that are linked together, as it were, in a chain leading, to cumulative, often formal, grounded theory (Stebbins, 1992a; 2001b; in press). Studies near the beginning of the chain are wholly or predominantly exploratory in scope. Each study, or link, in the chain examines or, at times, reexamines a related group, activity, or social process or aspect of a broader category of groups, activities, and so on.

Where this metaphor of a chain of studies becomes inadequate is in its failure to suggest the accretive nature of properly executed, concatenated exploration. In the metaphor of the chain each link is equally important.

Whereas in scientific concatenation the studies in the chain are not only linked, they are also predicated on one another. That is later studies are guided, in significant measure, by what was found in earlier research in the same area as well as by the methods used and the samples examined there. Thus each link plays a somewhat different part in the growing body of research and in the emerging grounded theory. It is important to note, too, that the earlier studies only *guide* later exploration; they do not control it to the point where discovery becomes hedged in by preconceptions.

The studies reported in the present chapter, many of them exploratory, are however, concatenating in a special way. More precisely they have steered aspects of the serious leisure perspective in dramatically new directions, namely, into another field of research. This is, to be sure, continued exploration (where such work is properly open-ended), but now, the choice of research subject springs from a desire to link the Perspective with another scholarly domain rather than to continue extending it within the ambit of one or more of the three forms, considered for purposes of this discussion as constituting a distinctive field of research. Theoretic elaboration is a deductive extension across the boundary separating two fields that has often been followed up in the new intellectual territory with, quite appropriately (continued), inductive, exploratory research.

I will introduce the works reviewed in this chapter in rough chronologic order, according to when the interdisciplinary extension was first made. Discerning these links is, itself, an act of discovery, albeit one that seems most often to be serendipitous, standing in contrast to the exploratory work that commonly follows (on the distinction between exploration and serendipity, see Stebbins, 2001c, pp. 3-4). We start with the link to tourism. As in chapter 2, to be considered for this review, each work discussed must center substantially, if not wholly, on one, two, or all three forms composing the serious leisure perspective.

Tourism

Hall and Weiler (1992, pp. 8-9) forged a close link with the serious leisure perspective when they demarcated "special interest tourism" according to five of the six distinguishing qualities and several of the durable benefits of serious leisure. They omitted only perseverance, a quality I nevertheless reinstated later (Stebbins, 1996c). Additionally, Hall (1992, pp. 147-149), in a separate chapter on sport and tourism, distinguished between players of and activity participants in sport tourism, relegating to the realm of casual leisure those who simply travel to watch sporting events.

My position is that the liberal arts hobby is the classificatory home of cultural tourism, which stands in contradistinction to that of recreational tourism (Stebbins, 1996c). The latter, in harmony with Delbaere's (1994) definition of it, is expressed in the other types of hobbies, principally activity participation and sports and games, as well as in amateur sport. As indicated in chapter 1, reading, chiefly in books, magazines, and newspapers, is the principal way in which most hobbyists acquire their liberal arts knowledge. But reading can be substantially augmented by, among other ways, participating directly in activities related to the pastime. This is certainly true for the cultural tourist who, in fact, may consider reading and travelling as equally enjoyable and important, if he or she does not regard the first as augmenting the second.

Still, some cultural tourism cannot be considered a hobby. Whether travel for the purposes of direct participation qualifies as a hobby, as serious leisure, depends in part on the pursuit of knowledge there being both systematic and enduring. A hobby is sustained over many years, not merely for two or three weeks of holiday time. From the participant's perspective, the vast majority of serious leisure pursuits unfold within the framework of a leisure role and its accompanying career as centered on the acquisition of skill, knowledge, or experience or a combination of these three. Such a career requires no small amount of time to take root and grow. An intense interest in an amateur, hobbyist, or volunteer activity motivates the enthusiast to use this time to pursue such leisure and the leisure career it offers. Consequently, people who participate in only one or two cultural tours, possibly separated by several years, who might nonetheless be classified in surveys as cultural tourists cannot, however, be classified in theory as hobbyists. Rather, such people are most accurately labelled *cultural dabblers*, a genre of casual leisure participant.

Cultural tourism, pursued as it is as serious leisure, results in a special identity (Stebbins, 1997e). This identity is special because it is based on the other five qualities of such leisure, none of which is found in casual leisure and mass tourism. Casual tourism, although hardly humiliating or despicable, is nonetheless too fleeting, mundane, and commonplace for most tourists to find much of an identity within it. Thus, when Urry (1994, p. 235) observes that modern identities are formed through play and consumption and expressed at times in touristic activity, we must always ask whether the tourism in question is mass or cultural.

The identity base of mass vis-à-vis cultural tourism is substantially different, giving those who go in for the latter an identity of far greater depth and complexity than the identity available to those who go in for the former. Mass tourism, by its very definition, is socially, financially, and geographically accessible to great numbers of people, as seen for example in much of guided tourism and camper tourism. By contrast, the objects attracting the cultural tourist are socially and psychologically much less accessible, for they require the development of certain tastes (e.g., in art, food, music, or architecture), acquisition of certain kinds of knowledge (e.g., a foreign language, the history of a region or country), or development of particular social skills (e.g., how to talk with the locals, how to act according to their norms).

In chapter 2 we covered Wearing's (2004) conceptualization of volunteer tourism and serious leisure, wherein career volunteering enables cultural understanding and elaboration of its potential benefits. Such tourism is sustainable because its impact is minimal, because it is typically small in scale while requiring little specialized infrastructure. Furthermore it therefore causes little damage to the environment on which ecotourism and other forms of tourism depend heavily. At the same time, as serious leisure, it contributes mightily to personal development (Wearing, 2001). Wearing and Neil (2001, p. 237) present a conceptual scheme relating serious leisure and volunteering to alternative tourism and its several types (one being cultural tourism). They also show mass tourism—casual leisure—partially overlapping the alternative form and its types.

Harrison (2001) presents a unique study of tourism as casual leisure. Her study of thirty-five upper middle-class Canadian tourists focused on the intense sensual pleasure that they derived from their travels. She concluded that tourism, even the casual leisure variety, may be much more than a banal escape, or vulgar consumption, as it is sometimes portrayed in the academic literature. Here casual leisure is more complex than meets the eye, though I would add, probably never as complex as typical serious, or even much of project-based, leisure.

Ethnicity

This link got its start in my zeal for learning Canada's other official language—French. Living, as I do, in Western Canada where French is a minority tongue, required that I somehow enhance my learning of it through routine direct contact in French with local francophones. The means to this end, for me, was to mount an exploratory study, in which I directly observed activities in the Calgary francophone community and interviewed a sample of its members (reported in Stebbins, 1994). This aspect of Canadian society had been heretofore almost totally neglected.

The decision to conduct this research was serendipitous, but discovery of the prominent played role by leisure there was one of the many fruits of the ensuing exploration.

Research (Stebbins, 1994; 1998d) suggests that French-speaking Canadians spend, in French, significant amounts of leisure time expressed in all three forms in, for example, singing in a chorale or acting in a play (amateurism), skiing with family or hiking with friends (hobbyist activity), or attending a dinner party or meeting for drinks with friends (casual leisure). Some activities are carried out in the world of formal groups and organizations, as theatrical work and choral singing are; some are carried out in the informal world of friendship networks and family relations as exemplified by going on a picnic and watching a French film. There is considerable francophone volunteering as well, exemplified in serving as organizer of the annual provincial francophone weekend get together (it resembles a community fair) or the annual local "sugar shack" (*cabane-à-sucre*) (both are project-based leisure). Francophone community centers rely heavily on casual volunteers to serve food, take tickets, vend drinks, sell crafts or baked goods, and similar functions. And, as noted in chapter 3, Canada-wide francophone games are held annually; they offer abundant opportunities for project-based volunteering (Gravelle and Larocque, 2005) as well as for competing in a large variety sporting events.

Turning to another facet of ethnicity, VandeSchoot (2005) studied a sample of Muslims in Calgary, to explore how Islam and leisure mix. She found that this religion strongly influenced their perceptions, preferences, and choices of leisure. Serious leisure was found to be acceptable often, because it squared with Islamic doctrine stating that Muslims should strive to find fulfillment in daily life. Much of casual leisure, on the other hand, was looked on as frivolous and contrary to their religious principles. All in the sample regarded their religious practices as obligatory, though some found them enjoyable as well—in effect leisure.

This is, of course, but a mere start of an extension into a very complex area of social life. The Perspective can help explain leisure and its place in the lives of minority racial, linguistic, religious, and national groups in society, but much exploratory research remains to be done to demonstrate in detail how this works.

Quality of Life and Well-Being

In conceptualizing quality of life, I use the subjective "want-based" approach (as opposed to the objective "social indicators" approach). The

want-based approach consists of four components: "a sense of achievement in one's work, an appreciation of beauty in nature and the arts, a
feeling of identification with one's community, a sense of fulfillment of
one's potential" (Campbell, Converse, and Rogers, 1976, p. 1).

Where does the serious leisure perspective fit in this scheme? Of the
three forms, serious leisure, itself, meets best the four components. The
first—sense of achievement—is evident in serious leisure from what was
said earlier about its rewards of personal enrichment, self-expression,
group accomplishment and contribution to the maintenance and development of the group as well as its qualities of career, effort, benefits, and
perseverance that people can routinely find here. The second component,
which refers to appreciation of beauty in nature and the arts, is found in
such serious leisure forms as the outdoor activities and artistic pursuits,
including backpacking, cross-country skiing, sculpting and playing string
quartets. Third, all serious leisure has links with the wider community,
if in no other way, than through the social worlds of its participants.
Additionally however, many serious leisure activities relate directly to
the larger community, as through artistic performances by amateurs,
interesting displays by hobbyists (of, for example, stamps, model trains,
show dogs), and needed services by volunteers. Sense of fulfilment of
potential—the fourth component—comes primarily from experiencing
the reward of self-actualization, but also, to a certain extent, from two
qualities of serious leisure, namely, finding a career in the activity and
having occasionally to persevere at following it.

These four components can also be realized in many leisure projects,
but the good quality of life found there will be more evanescent, and
possibly not even as sharply felt, as in the enduring pursuit of a serious
leisure activity. Casual leisure, too, can help generate a decent quality
of life, although primarily by appreciating beauty in nature and the arts
(e.g., subtype of sensory stimulation) and identifying with one's community (e.g., subtype of casual volunteering)

High quality of life, however generated, is a state of mind, which
to the extent people are concerned with their own well-being, must be
pursued with notable diligence. (Did we not speak earlier of career and
perseverance?) Moreover, high quality of life does not just "fall into one's
lap," as it were, but roots in desire, planning, and patience, as well as a
capacity to seek deep satisfaction through experimentation with all three
forms of leisure to eventually carve out an optimal leisure lifestyle. Personal agency is the watchword here. And we will see shortly that leisure
educators, leisure counsellors among them, can advise and inform about

a multitude of leisure activities that hold strong potential for elevating quality of life, but, in the end, it is the individual who must be motivated to pursue them and develop a plan for doing this.

Keyes (1998, p. 121) defines *social well-being* as the "absence of negative conditions and feelings, the result of adjustment and adaptation to a hazardous world." For him well-being, though a personal state, is influenced by a variety of social conditions, all of which are considered in the serious leisure perspective. Though the relationship is probably more complex than this, for purposes of the present discussion, let us incorporate in the following proposition what has been said in this section to this point: social well-being emanates from a high quality of life, as generated by some combination of serious leisure balanced with one or both of the other two forms.

Still, a major question remains: can even a serious leisure activity, which is not coerced, engender well-being when it is also engenders certain costs and occupies a marginal status with reference to the three social institutions of work, leisure, and family? The answer is, tentatively, yes it can. For, to the extent that well-being is fostered by fulfillment through life's ordinary activities, research evidence suggests that it is an important by-product of serious leisure (Haworth, 1986; Haworth and Hill, 1992; Mannell, 1993). As additional evidence the respondents in my several studies of serious leisure, when interviewed, invariably described in detail and with great enthusiasm the profound fulfillment they derived from their amateur, hobbyist, and volunteer activities.

All this evidence is, however, only correlational. No one has yet carried out a properly controlled study expressly designed to ascertain whether long-term involvement in a form of serious leisure actually leads to significant and enduring increases in feelings of well-being. The extent to which serious leisure can generate major interpersonal role conflict for some practitioners—it led to two divorces among the twenty-five respondents in a study of amateur theater (Stebbins, 1979, pp. 81-83; on family conflict in running, see also Goff, Flick, and Oppliger, 1997) —should be warning enough to avoid postulating an automatic link between serious leisure, on the one hand, and well-being, on the other. I also have anecdotal evidence that serious leisure activities can generate intrapersonal conflict, such as when people fail to establish priorities among their many and varied leisure interests or among those interests and their devotee work. This implies that even an approach-approach conflict between cherished leisure activities may possibly affect unfavorably well-being. Hamilton-Smith (1995, pp. 6-7) says our lack of knowledge about the link between serious leisure and well-being is a major lacuna in contemporary leisure research.

Leisure Education

Leisure education, which has been, for many years, a prominent branch of leisure studies, is itself a hybrid entity, with a leg in leisure studies and one in the field of education. Charles Brightbill was one of the first scholars to acknowledge the importance of what he variously called "education for leisure" and "leisure education." He wrote: "when we speak . . . of education for leisure, we have in mind the process of helping *all* persons develop appreciations, interests, skills, and *opportunities* that will enable them to use their leisure in personally rewarding ways" (italics in original, Brightbill, 1961, p. 188). Given these words, I think it safe to say that, were Brightbill writing today, he would argue that leisure education should center for the most part on either serious leisure or project-based leisure, if not both. In particular, such education should consist mainly of imparting knowledge about the nature of these two forms, about their costs and rewards, and about participating in particular leisure activities of this sort. This conception of leisure education (though without reference to project-based leisure), as initially set out (Stebbins, 1999), intentionally excluded casual leisure, on grounds that such leisure requires little or no training or encouragement to engage in it and find enjoyment there.

Yet, at various points in this book I have brought up the subject of optimal leisure lifestyle, which certainly grants notable importance to casual leisure. In line with this thinking the goal of leisure education, as just presented, should be rephrased: that goal should be to not only inform clients or students about the nature of casual leisure but also to inform them about its role in a well balanced, optimal leisure lifestyle. Leisure education includes helping people find the most appealing casual leisure available and effectively blend it with their serious and project-based leisure. In chapter 3 we reviewed the components of casual leisure that leisure educators need also to consider: its benefits (Stebbins, 2001b; Hutchinson and Kleiber, 2005) and its capacity for promoting relaxation (Kleiber, 2000).

Since the general public is largely unaware of the three forms of leisure, the first goal of educators for leisure, who when conceived of broadly include counsellors, volunteers, and classroom instructors, is to inform their clients or students about the nature and value of these three. Such information is important for anyone searching for an optimal leisure lifestyle. More particularly, such education should be composed of instruction on the nature of serious and project-based leisure, the general rewards (and costs) of such activity, the possibility of finding a leisure career in the first, and the variety of social and psychological advantages that can accrue to the person who pursues either of them (e.g., special identity, attractive routine and lifestyle, organizational belonging, central life interest, membership in a social world). In some instances, people will have to be told how to get started in the pursuits of interest to them. Elsewhere, I provide information on how to do this in North America (Stebbins, 1998a, chap. 6), which however, may sometimes be inappropriate for other parts of the world. Thus, to more effectively guide the people they are working with, leisure educators outside North America may have to gather information on how to get started that is specific to their country and local community.

Education is a complex process, with leisure education being no exception. Details on this process, as oriented by the serious leisure perspective, are found in Ruskin and Sivan (1995) and in Cohen-Gewerc and Stebbins (in press). A leisure education program for primary and secondary schools constructed along these theoretic lines, has been adopted in Israel, even though political upheavals there seem, so far, to have prevented its full implementation.

Gender

In the preceding chapter we explored gender as one of several concepts to be used to synthesize the serious leisure perspective. The purpose of the present section is to recognize formally that gender studies is a field of research in its own right, to which the Perspective has now been linked through diverse studies taking gender as a focal point of investigation. Raisborough (1999) was the first to do this, in her study of British sea cadets. She observed that research on serious leisure has tended to neglect the question of gendered experiences there, even creating the impression in some quarters that this form of leisure is a male only undertaking. Even though the involvements of women were explicitly described and analyzed in the fieldwork on stand-up comics (Stebbins, 1990) and barbershop singers (Stebbins, 1996a, chap. 6) and more sporadically explored in some of my other studies, her observation is nevertheless generally valid: there had been significant neglect of the question of gendered experiences in serious leisure. That is I had not gone to the field intentionally to study gender, as she did, but rather to study comedy, barbershop, and the like during the exploration of which gender emerged as an important issue for some of the interviewees.

Her investigation of amateurs in Britain's Sea Cadet Corps (SCC) shows how this neglect can obscure important data. One of her most intriguing findings was that, in the SCC, women more often than men failed to recognize its activities as a form of serious leisure. Instead, the regular routines of the SCC facilitated what these women defined as their own leisure, various forms of casual leisure involving neither the SCC nor their family or home. It was the regular routines of this organization that enabled these women to set aside time for a kind of leisure seen as rightfully theirs.

Retirement and Unemployment

In fact the earliest extension of the serious leisure perspective—done in the name of serious leisure—is nearly thirty years old. It outlined the many benefits of serious leisure for retirees (Stebbins, 1978a). I returned to this extension into the field gerontology twenty years later in a more global discussion of the place of serious leisure "after work" (Stebbins, 1998a). This book—*After work*—unlike the others I have written, is aimed at the educated lay public. Its mission is to inform them about serious and casual leisure and optimal leisure lifestyle, with emphasis, much as just discussed for leisure education, on the serious side. Practical in its orientation, it contains lists of suggested activities in all types and subtypes of serious leisure as well as numerous hints on how to get started in those that appeal to the reader.

After work is general, however; unemployment and retirement are occasionally mentioned, but the book mostly bears on free time wherever it is found in life (including after a day's work). Roger Mannell (1993), however, has specifically examined the role of serious leisure in retirement, providing thereby the backing of controlled research for my speculative claims made in 1978. He found that serious leisure and flow activities, appropriately organized for the elderly, can generate in them a great deal of enthusiasm.

Turning now to serious leisure and unemployment, we find that the relationship between the two is tentative. My review of the literature in this area reveals mixed findings (Stebbins, 2001a, pp. 126-127), with a few studies showing that some of the unemployed were bolstered during their months away from work by their serious leisure activities. Other studies, however, failed to find this effect. Clearly we need more research directly guided by the serious leisure perspective, where we can learn from respondents how they evaluate their leisure during this period of their lives and, to the extent they are involved in them, how they evaluate the three forms. Serious leisure is anything but trivial, but it is also self-interested, and given its magnetic, appeal could prevent meeting obligations, including searching for work or being selective about the work accepted.

I also reviewed the literature on retirement and serious leisure (Stebbins, 2001a, pp. 127-132), so that only work done since that date need be mentioned here. In that review I noted the special importance to the elderly of career and casual volunteering as well as the liberal arts hobbies. On the policy level, Kelly (1997, p. 177) proposes that retirees be encouraged to try to "direct their lives in a balance of engagement that is at least relatively satisfying." To be sure, this assumes adequate health, income, companionship, and transportation. It also assumes that the elderly know there are leisure activities that can be seriously pursued, a tall order perhaps, since a Canadian study suggests that they see leisure chiefly in casual terms (Roadburg, 1985, p. 69). Once again we see the importance of leisure education in promulgating the serious leisure perspective. Every segment of the population would seem to benefit from learning about it.

But, when the aforementioned conditions of adequate health, income, and so on are met, evidence continues to mount showing that older people are willing and able to pursue a wide variety of serious leisure activities (e.g., Stebbins, 2005d; Heuser, 2005; Roberson, 2005) and through it attain a higher level of fulfilment in life than otherwise. Furthermore Stebbins (2000d) concluded that retired professionals are especially likely to seek serious leisure in their postretirement years. Kelly (1993, p. 177) observes that "the process of constriction that characterizes later life may at least be delayed by opportunities that are both possible and satisfying."

Adult Education and Self-Directed Learning

Since I have examined elsewhere in detail (Stebbins, 2001a, pp. 94-102) the link between adult education and leisure, we need here only describe, in broad terms, this link. This will set the stage for a longer discussion on lifelong learning and the serious leisure perspective. As a guide for this chapter, we will use the definition of adult education prepared by UNESCO:

Adult education is the entire body of organized educational processes, whatever the content, level and method, whether formal or otherwise, whether they prolong or replace initial education in schools, colleges and universities as well as apprenticeship, whereby persons regarded as adult by the society to which they belong develop their abilities, enrich their knowledge, improve their technical or professional qualifications or turn them in a new direction and bring about changes in their attitudes or behavior in the twofold perspective of full personal development and participation in balanced and independent social, economic and cultural development. (UNESCO, 1976, p. 2)

Learning—adult learning in particular—is the object of these educational processes. "Continuing education" often refers to the same processes, although the idea usually connotes furthering a person's education beyond initial education undertaken as preparation for a work role (Jarvis, 1995, p 29).

In general, and in harmony with the emphasis in leisure education, adult education centers, for the most part, on serious rather than casual leisure. Such education can also be pursued, however, as a leisure project. For instance, amateurs in many arts and scientific fields avail themselves of adult education courses, and in the arts, even whole programs, that further their learning of a serious leisure activity. The same can be said for most of the individual amateur sports (e.g., golf, tennis, racquetball). Still, if we examine all the adult educational programs available in the typical North American city, it becomes clear that they ignore some amateur activities (e.g., handball, rodeo, weightlifting as well as auto and motorcycle racing and virtually all the entertainment arts, Stebbins, 2001a, p. 97).

Adult education is also, with the exception of collecting, a main avenue for learning hobbies. A great range of making and tinkering activities fill the multitude of North American adult education catalogs, including baking, decorating, do-it-yourself, raising and breeding, and various crafts (for a discussion of the many different hobbies, see Stebbins, 1998a, chap. 3). The same is true for activity participation, which includes such diverse enthusiasms as scuba diving, cross-country skiing, mushroom gathering, and ballroom dancing as well as a few of the hobbyist activities and sports and games (e.g., bridge, orienteering, and the martial arts). On the other hand the liberal arts hobbies are most often acquired purely through self-direction, chiefly by reading, as noted earlier. But here, too, we find exceptions, as in the general interest courses offered on certain arts, cultures, philosophies, and histories. Indeed, language instruction is one of the pillars of adult education.

Adult education courses related to volunteerism center mostly in such areas as fund raising, accounting and book-keeping, and management and recruitment of volunteers. To the extent that serious leisure volunteers are involved in these areas, they are likely to be interested in courses bearing on them. Still many career volunteers devote themselves to other tasks, which they learn outside the framework of adult education. That is, the group (club, society, association, organization) in which they serve provides the basic instruction they need to learn further while on the job.

Consonant with Houle's (1961) distinction between learning-oriented and goal-oriented motives for pursuing adult education is the fact that the liberal arts hobbies are the only form of serious leisure where learning is an end in itself. By contrast, amateurs, volunteers, and other hobbyists learn as a means to particular leisure ends, such as producing art, playing sport, collecting objects, or helping others. Sometimes both types of participant enrol in the same course, a pattern that may be especially common in science. Thus, some students in an adult education astronomy course may be liberal arts hobbyists, while others are there to learn about the heavens as background for their research.

Jones and Symon (2001) draw a similar distinction in their exploration of the implications of this difference for governmental policy in Britain. They note that adult education and lifelong learning offer resources oriented toward serious learning for six special groups: the unemployed, unwaged (volunteers), elderly, women, "portfolio workers" (hold many different jobs over a lifetime), and people with disabilities. Serious leisure offers an involving, fulfilling career to these groups that some members of them once had at work and other members of them never had there. Contemporary governmental policy in Britain (and, I would like to add, quite likely in all other Western countries) tends to overlook the existence of serious leisure and its implications for personal fulfillment, quality of life, and well-being.

Project-based leisure is what people are involved in when they take one or a few courses, with no intention of further involvement in the subject studied. Many a person has sat through one or two courses in an adult education program on astronomy, music appreciation, a genre of history, and the like simply for the pure satisfaction of learning something in these areas. Having learned what they set out to learn, they see that "project" as completed, and perhaps, move on to something else.

Self-Directed Learning

Roberson (2005, p. 205) notes the crucial differences between adult education and self-directed learning and then links the second to serious leisure. Drawing on an earlier conceptualization by Lambdin (1997), he says that "self-directed learning is intentional and self-planned learning where the individual is clearly in control of this process." Such learning may be formal (here it would be synonymous with adult education), but most often, it is informal. An important condition is that the learner controls the start, direction, and termination of the learning experience. Both adult education and self-directed learning are types of "lifelong learning." The latter is a broader idea than the first two, summarized by Selman and colleagues (1998, p. 21) as learning done throughout a person's lifetime, "from the cradle to the grave."

Roberson (2005) found that his sample of rural, elderly Americans (in the State of Georgia) took their learning seriously, as they pursued amateur, hobbyist, or volunteer roles. At the same time the respondents also said they "enjoyed" or had "fun" in these learning experiences. Roberson said they were "playful" when involved in them. In fact his findings would seem to lend empirical weight to the reward of self-gratification, where participants find a combination of superficial enjoyment and deep self-fulfilment.

Disabilities

The earliest work extending serious leisure into the field of disabilities was carried out by Kleiber and Patterson. Based on his research on people with spinal cord injuries, Kleiber (1996, p. 13) suggests that serious leisure activities could become an important element in the rehabilitation process of the disabled, possibly "by reconnecting with the self what was temporarily lost or in setting a new direction for a new self." Patterson (1997) forged an even more direct link between disability and serious leisure by explaining how the latter can serve as a nonpaying substitute for work for people whose disabilities force them into unemployment.

My work here has centered on the role leisure education can play in sensitizing specialists who work with people with disabilities as well as, of course, those very people (Stebbins, 2001a, pp. 96-102). Today, for most people with disabilities, leisure is predominantly casual. For this reason two kinds of serious leisure education are needed in this field. The first aims to educate or train people with disabilities to find satisfaction in an amateur, hobbyist, or career volunteer activity or in leisure projects of some sort. This kind of education involves informing them in detail, first, about one or more of the activities which appeal to them and for which their disabilities do not disqualify them and, then, about how to participate in those activities. In this regard, the liberal arts hobbies are possibly the most feasible sort of serious leisure for the largest number of people with disabilities.

The second kind of leisure education consists of instruction of a more general nature: informing people with disabilities about serious and project-based leisure as kinds of activity distinct from casual leisure. Here training is much the same for people with disabilities as for those without them. Since both the people with disabilities and the general public are largely unaware of the three forms of leisure, the first educational goal here must be to inform everyone about their nature and value. As already indicated, such information is important for anyone searching for an optimal leisure lifestyle.

Patterson has continued to work extending serious leisure into the field of disabilities studies and practice. For instance he recommended that community-based agencies serving people with disabilities implement leisure counselling and educational services as well as hire trained leisure counsellors to support their clients (Patterson, 2000). Given the subsequent addition of project-based leisure to the Perspective, I now add that form of leisure to this exhortation. In a later paper Patterson (2001) argues that we should build our leisure education programs for the intellectually disabled around serious leisure activities. Such activities can engender self-respect, self-esteem, and lead to greater acceptance by and social inclusion in the larger community. For the reason just given, we can also add project-based leisure to this suggestion.

Lee, McCormick, and Austin (2001, p. 29), writing on the theme of social inclusion in the larger community, note that serious leisure can help create and maintain meaningful interpersonal relationships, which can serve as a mechanism for integrating people with various kinds of disabilities into that community. Such leisure also provides a sense of belonging to the group, while possibly creating opportunities for assuming responsibilities and, as a result, feeling needed. As for project-based leisure here, it is probably less effective than in the previous circumstances. At least, to the extent that the project, though social, is still short (e.g., brief training period, brief period of service), enduring relationships will likely fail to develop.

Library and Information Science

Bates (1999, p. 1044) defines the field of library and information science (LIS) as "the study of the gathering, organizing, storing, retrieving, and dissemination of information." She points out that this field cuts across conventional academic disciplines, as its researchers engage in such "processes" as information seeking, teaching, and learning. This is done along lines of various "domains," or universes of recorded information, that are developed and retained for later access. LIS is both a pure science and a practical one, with the latter concentrated on developing services and products for specialties like journalism and library science.

Jenna Hartel has pioneered the extension of serious leisure into LIS. Hartel (2003) points out that, historically, LIS has leaned heavily toward studying scholarly and professional informational domains, while largely ignoring those related to leisure. In an attempt to help redress this imbalance, she introduces the study of information in hobbies. Serious leisure is examined for its library and informational forces and properties as these relate to a particular core leisure activity and the organizational milieu in which it is pursued. It is known that the patterns of storage, retrieval, and dissemination vary considerably from one core activity to another. Hartel is currently conducting research that explores these patterns in the hobby of cooking.

What about casual and project-based leisure and LIS? Some casual leisure is highly dependent on information, particularly, these days, information disseminated over the Internet. Thus, on the casual leisure side, mass tourism rests, in significant part, on information about touristic sites offered by travel agencies, magazines, and newspaper columns. The tribes described in chapter 4 offer another fertile arena for studying the role of information (much of it electronic) in casual leisure. And relevant information is gathered, organized, disseminated, and the like in some project-based leisure, as in certain one-shot volunteering and liberal arts projects and certain occasional projects.

Entertainment and Popular Culture

Elsewhere (Stebbins, in press) I present my extension of the serious leisure perspective into the field of the sociology of entertainment. A short resume of that statement is offered here. First I argue that two key concepts organize this branch of sociology. One—*entertainment*—can be defined as an object or occasion intentionally provided to a public for their enjoyment, or pleasure, that is meant to hold their attention for the period of time the object or occasion is perceived. That the entertainment may, for various reasons, flop with some or all members of the public, though an unhappy situation for the would-be entertainer, does not contradict this definition. For the *intention* had been to entertain. The second key concept—the *entertainer*—can be defined as a performer who, directly or indirectly (e.g., via film, TV, videotape), from a stage or its equivalent, provides entertainment to a public.

The consumers of entertainment, when truly entertained, are immersed in a leisure experience. In this instance the experience is primarily pleasurable, one of enjoyment and rather little else. Such leisure is casual. While the public of an entertainment form is enjoying itself in casual leisure, the producers of it are having a quite another experience. In this role they perform, each in his social world, as either amateurs or professionals and as either regulars or insiders. The amateurs, of course, are engaged in a form of leisure of their own, which however, is serious rather than casual.

We should recognize, as well, the existence of entertainment projects, with quite possibly, most of them being amateur in nature. The brief listing in chapter 3 of selected projects in entertainment theater exemplifies this form of leisure. Such projects may be more common than we realize. For instance, how often have you been treated to a slide or video show of a lengthy, exotic trip taken by a friend or relative?

Popular culture includes, in broadest scope, any cultural item that has achieved popularity, or that has developed a mass public. Whereas the overlap of entertainment and popular culture is considerable, it is, however, far from complete. For instance, smoking dope (deviant leisure) is entertaining but not a popular, widespread, practice. And numerous popular artifacts and practices exist that are decidedly not leisurely, among them, gasoline, toothpaste, queuing, and paying income tax.

The common domain occupied by both leisure and popular culture is nevertheless vast. Moreover the large majority of popular leisure activities can be qualified as casual rather than serious leisure. But the relationship between leisure and popular culture is complex, as table 5.1 shows.

Table 5.1
Relationship of Leisure and Popular Culture

Popular Culture	Consumption of Popular Culture	Production of Popular Culture
As Work	(1) Devotee work in sport and entertainment	(2) Professional work (full- and part-time) in sport and entertainment
As Leisure	(3) Casual leisure (7 types)	(4) Amateur sport and entertainment, Hobbies (displayable forms)

From: Stebbins, R.A. (2006c). Leisure and popular culture. In G. Ritzer (Ed.), *The Blackwell Encyclopedia of the Social Sciences*. Cambridge, MA: Blackwell.

The terms in this table are explained elsewhere in either the present chapter or chapter 1. Note in cell 1, however, that, with reference to the present discussion, popular culture workers meeting the criteria of occupational devotion (discussed in next section of present chapter) can be said to be both consumers and producers of their popular culture. Examples include pop music stars who find deep fulfillment while simultaneously making and listening to their music and commercial painters, writers, and filmmakers who, as they produce their works, enjoy the same kind of aesthetic experience.

Cell 3 of table 5.1 refers only to seven of the eight subtypes of casual leisure. The missing subtype is casual volunteering, omitted because volunteering of any kind occupies an indeterminate position in all this. Of the three types of serious leisure, it quite possibly draws the largest number of participants (no quantitative comparative data are available). It is also much talked about these days for its key role in creating and maintaining civil society and for its capacity to fill the gap left by business and government through their ongoing failure to deliver needed community services. Yet, apart from volunteering to help organize and run as leisure projects certain popular sports and arts events (e.g., Olympic Games, major arts festivals)—classifiable as an indirect contribution to producing these events—volunteering would appear to be yet another area where leisure and popular culture must be considered separate phenomenon (for further discussion of leisure and popular culture, see Stebbins, 2006c).

Other Extensions

It seems that the possibility for extending the serious leisure perspective is unending. At least I am still doing this, and yet, I am not laying awake nights looking for new extensions. Rather they just seem suddenly to come to mind. Four have recently captured my attention.

One of these is the link between serious leisure and work, where the line of reasoning runs from the first to the second. In the past it has been fashionable, at times, to discuss the obverse: how work influences leisure (remember the celebrated spillover and compensation hypotheses of the 1970s), which is not, however, the line of influence I want to discuss here. Rather, I finally came to grips (Stebbins, 2004b) with the observation made over the years by various people who have heard about serious leisure that some work is like leisure (read: serious leisure), that in such work the line between work and leisure is virtually erased. Here, because their jobs are so fulfilling, people are paid so that they may work. The argument set out in the above-mentioned reference is as follows: work in some of the liberal professions, counselling fields, skilled trades, and small businesses is essentially serious leisure, in which, nevertheless, the worker finds a livelihood, albeit by no means always a highly lucrative one. There may also be an extension into some forms of work from some kinds of project-based leisure, a possibility not addressed in Stebbins (2004b), but one certainly well worth exploring.

All three forms of the serious leisure perspective are evident in the question of the leisurely nature of shopping. Shopping has attracted a certain amount of scholarly attention—it is a scholarly field—some of which is reviewed in Stebbins (2006a). In that same article I also examine how shopping is sometimes obligation, sometimes serious leisure, sometimes casual leisure, and sometimes project-based leisure. Agreeable obligation and leisure combine when shopping for, say, a dress for a special reception (assuming one has the time and money for this activity). This is likely to be casual leisure, whereas the golfer shopping for a new and better set of clubs is engaging pleasant, obligatory (his old set was stolen) activity that is, in effect, part of his serious leisure. Shopping that, to be done effectively, requires substantial knowledge of the product and its market, whether as obligation or (serious) leisure, may be a source of pride. Window-shopping is, for the most part, casual leisure. And consider the sense of fulfillment some people experience in buying, for example, a new house or automobile. Assuming that they are not upset by the financial implications of such a purchase and that they have worked up a solid knowledge of the product and its market, carefully searching out the best buy and realizing the best deal can be deeply rewarding, however necessary (obligatory) that purchase for the buyer. This is shopping as project-based leisure.

We turn next to contemplation, which also relates to all three forms of the serious leisure perspective (for a more detailed statement of contemplation in casual and serious leisure, see Stebbins, 2006d). For our purposes, contemplation and reflection are treated as synonyms; both terms referring to the act of intensely thinking about something. When contemplating (reflecting) we make thought on a particular subject the center of our attention, the dominant activity of the moment. As an activity that endures over time, running in length from a few seconds to possibly an hour or more, it is however largely mental, even though the contemplator may manipulate related objects during this period. Contemplation may be intense and relatively impermeable, as expressed in the phrase "lost in thought," or it may be relatively permeable, where a person's thoughts are easily interrupted by environmental stimuli.

My informal observations suggest that contemplation comes in at least four types. One is *obligatory contemplation*, a process forced on us from time to time, as we try in certain areas of life (e.g., work, outside work) to solve problems from which we cannot escape. Two, *casual leisure contemplation* is, by contrast, not coerced, but is rather taken up as a form of casual leisure of the play variety. This is reflection, or speculation, purely for the fun of it. Three, there is also *serious and project-based leisure as contemplation*, or reflection devoted to solving a problem arising with regard to a serious leisure activity or a leisure project. Though not play, this is nevertheless uncoerced, in that the associated activity itself is uncoerced. This kind of reflection occurs when, for example, a participant ponders the best training approach for an upcoming marathon, considers which of two musical instruments to buy, or reflects on the pros and cons of a prospective volunteer role. Four, *contemplation as serious leisure* is the classificatory home of complex reflective activity engaged in for its own sake. The activity is complex, for if a participant is to learn how to execute it, he or she must acquire special skills and a body of knowledge to go with them. This type—sometimes called "meditation" —is exemplified by such systems as Yoga, Tai Chi, and Transcendental Meditation. Meditation, or contemplation, in search of spirituality as guided by Christian thought is a further example.

One further extension bears mentioning, namely, that of the fit of the serious leisure perspective in the field of arts administration. Most people who attend arts events (e.g., concerts, festivals, performances, exhibitions) or patronize arts facilities (e.g., galleries, museums, libraries) are seeking a leisure experience. Thus of use to arts administrators, whose job is, in part, to market the arts they have been hired to manage, is knowledge about this experience, particularly knowledge about its nature and its distribution in the population of potential arts buffs and consumers. I have explored elsewhere in greater depth (Stebbins, 2005e) how consumption of the arts is differently realized in three forms of leisure.

The relationship of serious and casual leisure to arts administration is set out in figure 5.1. This figure shows that some members of the public of an art observe it from their interest in serious leisure, whereas other members of that public are interested in it only as casual leisure. Figure 5.1 shows further that, as we have seen, the arts have many reasons to seek help from volunteers, who may serve there in career and casual volunteering roles. Conceived of prior to the idea of project-based leisure, this figure omits project-based volunteering in the arts, much of which is conducted during festivals, special exhibitions, special concerts, and similar one-shot events. This kind of volunteering, too, falls within the realm of arts administration.

Figure 5.1
Serious and Casual Leisure and Arts Administration

Figure 5.1

SERIOUS LEISURE

Public	**Volunteers**
Amateurs Hobbyists	examples:
│	- board member
│	- guide
Liberal Arts Buffs	- receptionist

Reward: deep fulfillment   deep fulfillment

CASUAL LEISURE

Public-Consumers	**Volunteers**
- sensory stimulation	examples:
- passive entertainment	- take/sell tickets
- active entertainment	- hand out programs
- relaxation	- give directions
- sociable conversation	- usher
- play	- serve drinks
	- stuff envelops

Reward: enjoyment   **enjoyment**

From: Stebbins, R.A. (2005). The role of leisure in arts administration. *Occasional Paper Series*, Paper No. 1. Eugene, OR: Center for Community Arts and Public Policy, University of Oregon. (published at: http://aad.uoregon.edu/icas/documents/ stebbins0305.pdf)

Conclusions

To date the serious leisure perspective has been extended into sixteen fields. In the large majority of these extensions, all three forms are centrally implicated as part of the extension itself, or less commonly, as backdrop (usually casual leisure) intended to show the limitations of the extension in question. It is clear, I believe, that the serious leisure perspective offers a far richer and more coherent view of leisure in related fields than would be available by extending only one or two of the three forms.

Furthermore, the rate of extension has increased over the years. According to my crude count, the number of extensions more than doubled in half the time between writing the *New Directions* book (Stebbins, 2001a) and the present volume compared with the number of extensions made between 2001 and the first stock-taking (Stebbins, 1992a). Presumably extension cannot occur indefinitely; there is a finite number of fields to which such intellectual reach will be valid. On the other hand, the process is still to run its full course, for there are some fields to which extension is obvious though yet to be effected. One of these is recreational therapy. Another is health. Apropos the latter, the chain of reasoning, in general, runs as follows: self-fulfillment, whether achieved through serious leisure or devotee work, leads to enhanced quality of life and well-being, and then, on to improved psychological health and physical health, to the extent the second is influenced by the first. This serious leisure-health link has not been formally explored, however, in that there is no publication on the matter. In brief no formal extension exists. We will take up this subject again in the final chapter.

Nor does an extension exist between the serious leisure perspective and the study of emotions, be they positive or negative. The link envisaged here is with the sociology and psychology of emotions. Certainly negative emotion can be felt in leisure, as in anger at an umpire's call in amateur baseball or embarrassment at having performed poorly in a local theater production. Among the costs of serious leisure are the negative emotional situations occasionally faced by participants.

To underscore and study the positive side of emotion and other personal states, a new field known as "positive psychology" has emerged within the discipline of psychology. Martin Seligman proposed the new area in his presidential address at the 1998 annual meeting of the American Psychological Association. Its link with the serious leisure perspective is obvious in several places in the following passage.

> I proposed changing the focus of the science [psychology] and the organization of scientists in the world. I proposed changing the focus of the science and the profession from repairing the worst things in life to understanding and building the qualities that make life worth living. ...I call this new orientation "Positive Psychology." At the subjective level, the field is about positive experience: well-being, optimism, flow, and the like. At the individual level it is about the character strengths— love, vocation, courage, aesthetic sensibility, leadership, perseverance, forgiveness, originality, future-mindedness, and genius. At the community level it is about the civic virtues and the institutions that move individuals toward better citizenship, responsibility, parenting, altruism, civility, moderation, tolerance, and work ethic (from Seligman's "Positive Psychology Network Concept Paper" found at: http://www.psych.upenn. edu/seligman/ppgrant.htm, p 3).

Seligman added that this new field is meant to develop into a "positive social science." This to counteract the fact that many other social science disciplines also emphasize the negative rather than the positive side of human life. Happily leisure studies is not guilty of this oversight—it is the only truly *happy science*, notwithstanding the little list of negative emotions presented in the previous paragraph. A formal link between the serous leisure perspective and positive psychology will be forged in July, 2006.[1]

Finally, note that all extensions considered in this chapter are partial. In each the link has been made, but many details about it remain to be worked out through research and further theorizing. To repeat my remarks made at the beginning of this chapter: theoretic elaboration is a deductive extension across the boundary separating two fields that has, as the preceding pages show, often been followed up in the new intellectual territory with, quite appropriately (continued), inductive, exploratory research.

Note

1.   I will present in July 2006 at the Third European Congress on Positive Psychology a keynote address relating the serious leisure perspective to positive psychology.

6

History of the Perspective

"I'm serious about my archaeology," exclaimed one amateur who had, for several years, been pursuing his science. "It's not like what most people do for leisure." An amateur baseball player told me that "what we are doing here is not church-league stuff. Many of us hope to be scouted by the pros and maybe get an offer." And from an amateur thespian: "community theater is good quality drama; it is not your typical high-school play or anything anywhere near that. That's because we take our acting seriously and work on perfecting our parts."

Out of remarks like these the term *serious leisure* was born, born between 1973 and 1976 while I was collecting data for what was to become the "fifteen-year project" of research on amateurs and professionals. It is, in effect, a folk term. For, directly or indirectly, many of the amateur interviewees (autobiographers, in the case of the library study of classical musicians) decisively distanced themselves from the dominant conception of leisure as "simply a good time," doing so by underscoring the seriousness with which they approached their avocational passion.

The Perspective: Its Early Days

It should be noted, at the outset, that parts of the serious leisure perspective had been discussed before, or were being discussed as, I entered this area. De Grazia, (1962, pp. 332-336), Glasser (1970, pp. 190-192), Kaplan (1975, pp. 80, 183), and Kando (1980, p. 108) have all recognized the distinction between serious and casual leisure, even if they used different adjectives. In a far more simplistic way than suggested now by the serious leisure perspective, the first three leaned toward serious leisure as the ideal way for people in postindustrial society to spend their free time.

Personal Background

A while ago (Stebbins, 2000e) I undertook a contextual analysis of serious leisure, with the intention of viewing the field through the critical lens of the sociology of knowledge. Part of that analysis bore on the "existential basis" of serious leisure, which I recapitulate here as background for understanding my place in the rise of the serious leisure perspective.

The social and cultural bases of serious leisure, as an idea, can be examined from two angles: my position as its first and principal architect and the positions of the people who pursue it. I consider first my own position. In standard demographic terms, I am a white, male, Protestant, upper middle-class naturalized Canadian of American birth and upbringing, whose adult work life has unfolded almost entirely as a professor in sociology departments in three North American universities and an undergraduate college. I was thirty-six years old when I started studying amateurs and was, at the time, an amateur musician. Earlier I had been a professional musician, and still earlier a university-level athlete. Shortly thereafter I developed an avid interest in cross-country skiing and mountain "scrambling," or hiking without technical equipment to mountain peaks and ridges.

Culturally speaking, my values include those of achievement, self-development, and self-expression, which I have realized equally through work and leisure. As mentioned, I have worked and pursued my leisure in the North American milieu, one where work has generally been more highly valued than leisure and where the latter is generally equated with casual leisure, with most people knowing little about its serious counterpart. Nevertheless, the clamor has grown louder in the past twenty-five years among government officials and health and lifestyle specialists here and in many other parts of the western world for participation by the general public in physical leisure and exercise and, in some quarters, even in nonphysical serious leisure. It remains to be seen, however, how much actual change in leisure habits will ultimately flow from these pronouncements. At least research in the United States gives little cause for optimism with respect to physical leisure, most of which is serious, for Robinson and Godbey (1997, p. 184) report that people of all walks of life have been less active during the 1990s than earlier.

The majority of my respondents in all the many serious leisure activities I have studied (I have studied nineteen, most of which are mentioned in this chapter) fit reasonably well my own sociocultural profile, except that, where appropriate, many were female while very few were university professors, had worked in both Canada and the United States, and had my serious leisure interests. Moreover, all age groups were represented, albeit with noticeable variation from activity to activity. And whereas I never asked respondents about their religion, I suspect that the ratio of Protestants, Catholics, and Jews in my samples was about the same as in the general population. Also of interest is the fact that each activity studied attracted a number, although always a minority, of working-class and lower-level white-collar enthusiasts who commonly participated easily with their upper-middle-class colleagues and who were universally evaluated largely, if not entirely, on their ability in and commitment to their leisure. Neither ability nor commitment was correlated with class in my samples.

The Fifteen-Year Project

If I had to identify one day on which the fifteen-year project commenced, I would have to select a day in early January of 1974. For it was during that month that I began the library research that eventually led to a paper on amateur musicians written for presentation at a conference the following spring. Having been involved in amateur music for most of my life (except for a two-year interlude as a professional), I was well aware that participants in that field regarded amateurism as something special. That January day marked my first academic opportunity to study amateur music systematically and to record some of my thoughts that had been collecting on the subject over the years.

My plan was to write an ethnographic paper on amateur classical musicians, based on my own experience as well as on the biographic, autobiographic, and philosophic literature that touches on these musicians' social lives. That I did. In fact, I wrote and subsequently published three papers (Stebbins, 1976; 1978b; 1978c). Yet, in retrospect, these were the least significant events in those early months of 1974.

What was most significant was my realization that neither sociology nor any other discipline had developed a substantial definition of amateur. (The closest anyone came to such a definition was Elizabeth Todd [1930], who wrote a largely historical article on amateurism.) I discovered this conceptual deficiency during my search for a definition with which to organize my ideas and observations on amateurs in music. The search was in vain. Nevertheless, it compelled me to meet the problem head-on; to develop my own definitions of amateur, the results of which appeared in chapter 1. But there were other consequences as well.

The lack of a social science definition of amateurs meant that no one had actually conceived of them in the light in which they are examined here: as people occupying a unique, marginal position, or role, within contemporary North American society. To be sure, amateur groups had been studied, but their status as amateurs in the community had never been the object of these investigations. That is, they were ignored as participants in leisure. Moreover, the groups studied have nearly always consisted of adolescents or children, for whom the consequences of pursuing a form of serious leisure differ greatly from those for adults.

It became clear, too, that amateurs are found throughout art, science, sport, and entertainment; that they can be distinguished, by a variety of criteria, from professionals who work in the same field and from dabblers who merely play at it; and that we should know much more about, seemingly, one of the most complicated and neglected facets of modern leisure. So I set to work to design a crucial research project, one that would help answer many of the questions raised by my preliminary theoretic efforts with the musical autobiographies.

By spring of 1975, I had obtained the necessary funding to conduct an exploratory study of amateurism in the Dallas/Fort Worth area. It was a one-year project centering on amateurs in theater, archaeology, and baseball. From it I learned, among many other things, that it was a mistake to study amateurs to the exclusion of their professional counterparts. I also learned that, if my explorations were to have true scientific value, I would have to study at least two examples in each of the aforementioned areas in which amateurs and professionals exist and are linked to one another. By the end of 1976, then, I had completed the first four of this octet of studies (the fifteen-year project). This included my own participant-observational experience in the world of amateur classical music and a review of over 200 biographic, autobiographic, and philosophic accounts in a field in which, unlike the other seven studies, I was, as Adler and Adler (1987) put it, a "complete-member-researcher."

Following my relocation to the University of Calgary, I launched into a similar exploration of Canadian astronomers, this time, however, at both levels. That study was conducted from late 1977 through early 1978. Then came my first contact with amateurs and professionals in the entertainment field. That was in the first half of 1979, when I undertook the study of magicians. Later, in 1983 and 1984, I returned to the field to examine a second sport; Canadian football. Later still came the study of stand-up comics, my second and final entertainment field. These final four studies, unlike the first four, were based largely on Canadian samples (some American professional comics and football players working in Canada were also interviewed).

All this research, along with two conceptual statements, formed the basis for a set of generalizations reported in various books and articles and summarized in Stebbins (1992a), the latter signaling the end of the fifteen-year project. I list below, in abbreviated form and by type of leisure participant, the publications that emerged from the fifteen-year project. They are fully referenced in the References section. From here on, when I discuss in general terms the eight types of participants, separately or in combinations, I will do so under the heading of the "Project."

THEORETIC STATEMENTS

- The amateur; Two sociological definitions, *Pacific Sociological Review*
- Serious leisure: A conceptual statement, *Pacific Sociological Review*

CLASSICAL MUSICIANS

- Music among friends: The social network of amateur classical musicians, *International Review of Sociology* (Series II)
- Classical music amateurs: A definitional study, *Humboldt Journal of Social Relations*
- Creating high culture: The American amateur classical musician, *Journal of American Culture*

ACTORS

- *Amateurs: On the margin between work and leisure*
- Family, Work, and amateur acting. In *Social research and cultural policy*

ARCHEOLOGISTS

- *Amateurs: On the margin between work and leisure*
- Avocational science: The avocational routine in archaeology and astronomy, *International Journal of Comparative Sociology*
- Science a*mators*? Rewards and costs in amateur astronomy and archaeology, *Journal of Leisure Research*

BASEBALL PLAYERS

- *Amateurs: On the margin between work and leisure*

ASTRONOMERS

- Avocational science: The avocational routine in archaeology and astronomy, *International Journal of Comparative Sociology*
- Science a*mators*? Rewards and costs in amateur astronomy and archaeology, J*ournal of Leisure Research*
- Amateur and professional astronomers: A study of their inter-relationships, *Urban Life*

ENTERTAINMENT MAGICIANS

- *The magician: Career, culture, and social psychology in a variety art*

FOOTBALL PLAYERS

- *Canadian football: The view from the helmet*

STAND UP COMICS

- *The laugh-makers: Stand-up comedy as art, business, and life-style*

Early in the Project it became clear to me, as it already was to my research participants, that leisure can be conceived of in two great forms: serious and casual. *Casual leisure* is not, however, a folk term. Rather, I coined it. The participants nevertheless gave it both credence and validity, by pointing out that their serious leisure was extraordinary activity, unlike what most everyone else does in their free time. Other adjectives might have served as well as that of "casual," but I settled on it as being as good a label as any for summarizing what they felt about the many forms of popular leisure of the day. In 1982 I formally wrote, for the first time, defining and linking both terms in the concept of serious leisure (Stebbins, 1982a).

Furthermore it became evident toward the end of the Texas research that hobbyists and volunteers were, in many ways, like amateurs, but at the same time, they were people filling different, albeit equally distinct, roles. Indeed the amateurs in the Project sometimes referred to themselves as hobbyists or volunteers, and I was accustomed to similar confusion in amateur classical music circles (one of my own leisure passions) and in the related autobiographic literature that I had read. It was further evident that leisure of this complex sort—serious leisure—was being overlooked by social scientists. To be sure there were studies of amateurs, which as already noted here, centered on matters other than their distinctive role and status in free time, in the world of leisure. The same was true for research on volunteers, while hobbyists were virtually ignored altogether.

Exploring Serious Leisure

The gauntlet was down. I already had experience conducting qualitative/exploratory research in two other, quite different fields (i.e., education and deviance). I had been guided in both by Glaser and Strauss's (1967) manual on grounded theory. From this experience I realized that, to develop reasonably valid, generalizable, inductive theory, I would need more data than the four studies I had carried out could provide. Accordingly I made the decision, shortly after I moved to Calgary, to continue on, to carry out the Project.

A number of people have asked why I chose the particular mix of fields that I did. My justification is partly practical. For various reasons, both financial and academic, the studies had to be carried out close to home. I had therefore to draw on fields that were sufficiently represented locally. But I also wanted to look at established amateur groups, so that initially, at least, the difficulties of becoming established could be avoided. They could always be scrutinized later. I further decided that, where possible, my focus would be on collective amateurism, as opposed to individual amateurism (e.g., painting, writing, playing golf or tennis), so that I could examine the extensive effects of social interaction and group culture and structure. Again, the individual forms could always be dealt with at some other time. Also, because I prefer to collect my own data, I could only study the groups in tandem. Finally, I decided I had to get away from music, with which I have an insider's familiarity, and study other fields that I knew initially only as an outsider. The amateur groups mentioned earlier met these diverse considerations.

The methodology throughout the project has been qualitative, the exploratory research approach initially set out by Glaser and Strauss (1967) and more recently elaborated by Glaser (1978) and myself (Stebbins, 2001c). In general, I first observed extensively the routine activities of each amateur-professional combination. As I became acquainted with their lifestyles, I embarked on lengthy, semistructured, face-to-face interviews, in most instances with samples of thirty amateur and another thirty professional respondents. To the extent warranted by their lifestyles, social worlds, and core activities, I asked similar questions of the respondents in all fields; I felt I would then be in a better position to generalize across them. Each field is unique, however, demanding some special observing, analyzing, interviewing, probing, and reporting of its distinctive aspects. The result was a significant measure of "substantive grounded theory" (Glaser and Strauss, 1967, pp. 33-35) for each field studied.

Based on this substantive grounded theory I develop in somewhat more abstract terms, a "formal grounded theory" (as Glaser and Strauss put it) of serious leisure (Stebbins, 2001a) and, in the present book of the serious leisure perspective as it links together the three forms. In constructing these formal theories I learned, first hand, about the importance of concatenating research through exploration. The expression *concatenated exploration* refers at once to a longitudinal research process and the resulting set of open-ended studies that are linked together, as it were, in a chain leading, to cumulative, often formal, grounded theory (my most up-to-date discussion of this process is found in Stebbins, 2006b). Studies near the beginning of the chain are wholly or predominantly exploratory in scope. Each study, or link, in the chain examines or, at times, reexamines a related group, activity, or social process or aspect of a broader category of groups, activities, and so on.

Where this metaphor of a chain of studies breaks down, is in its failure to suggest the accretive nature of properly executed, concatenated exploration. In the metaphor of the chain each link is equally important. Whereas in scientific concatenation the studies in the chain are not only linked, they are also predicated on one another. That is later studies are guided, in significant measure, by what was found in earlier research in the same area as well as by the methods used and the samples examined there. Thus each link plays a somewhat different part in the growing body of research and in the emerging grounded theory. Furthermore note that the earlier studies only *guide* later exploration; they do not control it to the point where discovery is thwarted by preconceptions.

Since the study of serious leisure has now taken off in many other parts of the Western world, this conceptual development holds for Western leisure life outside North America, where it was originally pioneered.

After the Project

Publication of *Amateurs, professionals, and serious leisure* in 1992 signaled the culmination of the Project. It also served as the first stocktaking of the field of serious leisure as it had developed to that time. And just as important that occasion also dramatically highlighted, at least for me, the need to explore, in similar open-ended fashion, the other two types of serious leisure. I started first on the hobbies, though study of them got underway in unusual fashion. While the Project was being carried out, I was simultaneously leading, from time to time beginning in 1979, participants in a travel-study course that I taught on New Orleans to that city to experience a special kind of cultural tourism. I came to realize that those participants were, what I would later write about as, "liberal arts hobbyists" (Stebbins, 1994a). Discussions with them, combined with my knowledge of the culture of the "City that Care Forgot," eventuated in publication of *The Connoisseur's New Orleans* (Stebbins, 1995). Still, this was not the first statement on hobbies guided by the serious leisure side of the Perspective.

For much earlier Snyder (1986) had examined elderly shuffleboard players, classifiable in the serious leisure perspective as sports and games hobbyists. Allan Olmsted (e.g., 1988; 1991; 1993) had already been conducting research from this conceptual angle on collectors of guns and certain other objects. About the same time Mittelstaedt (1990-91; 1995) published his work on Civil War reenactments, valuable in part, for its examination of mixed hobbies (e.g., a participant who makes a period uniform (hobby subtype of making and tinkering) and then, dressed in it, fights a mock battle (hobby subtype of activity participation). The hobbyist sport of curling was studied by Apostle (1992) and the game of contract bridge by Scott and Godbey (1992; 1994). Lambert (e.g., 1995; 1996) has looked extensively at genealogy, a liberal arts hobby. Yair (1990; 1992) did research on Israeli runners, some of whom, contrary to the serious leisure perspective, he classified as amateurs. His primary interest revolved around levels of commitment to the hobby shown by different groups of runners. Somewhat later Hastings and colleagues (1995) and Hastings, Kurth, and Schloder (1996), in a comparative study of Americans and Canadians, applied the Perspective to the careers of masters swimmers.

About this time came publication of *The Barbershop Singer* (Stebbins, 1996a), an exploratory study of male and female singers in Calgary. Barbershop can be classified as activity participation. Shortly thereafter, Baldwin and Norris (1999) studied the American Kennel Club, and the making and tinkering hobby of breeding purebred dogs. Some of these hobbyists also train or show their animals, sometimes doing both. More recently King (2001) has contributed to the literature with a study of quilting. And, most recently, Stebbins (2005c) wrote about the hobbyist mountain sports of kayaking, snowboarding, and mountain and ice climbing. All these studies, in addition to their many other contributions, provide rich descriptions of the complex core activities around which they revolve.

Amateurs

Even during the years of the Project I was not alone in studying ama-teurs. Thus Etheridge and Neapolitan (1985) examined a sample of craft artists in the United States. Their data showed that amateurs are more serious about craft work than dabblers, as measured by amount of training and propensity to read craft magazines. Furthermore, the dabblers saw this leisure as recreation, as diversion from their daily routine, whereas the amateurs saw it as something more profound, as an expression of a strong commitment to perfection and artistic creativity.

Much later Yoder (1997) explored tournament bass fishing in the United States, where he learned that, first, fishers here are amateur sports enthusiasts, not hobbyists (contrary to my earlier classification of them as "activity participants," Stebbins, 1992, p. 12). Second, he found that commodity producers serving both amateur and professional tournament fishers play a role significant enough to require modifying the original tri-angular model of professional-amateur-public (P-A-P) system of relation-ships first set out in Stebbins (1979). In other words, in the social world of these amateurs, some strangers are highly important; they consist, in the main, of national fishing organizations, tournament promoters, and manufacturers and distributors of sporting goods and services. Significant numbers of amateurs make, sell, or advertise commodities for the sport. And professional fishers are supported by commodity agents by means of paid entry fees for tournaments, provision of boats and fishing tackle, and subsidies for living expenses. Top professionals are paid a salary to promote fishing commodities. As discussed in chapter 1, Yoder's (1997, p. 416) modification has resulted in a more complicated triangular model, consisting of a system of relationships between commodity agents, pro-fessionals/commodity agents, and amateurs/publics (C-PC-AP).

About the same time Juniu, Tedrick, and Boyd (1996) examined amateur and professional orchestral musicians in the United States. The authors found that the amateurs did not see their performances as "pure leisure" nor did the professionals see them as "pure work." In fact, the views of the two differed little in this regard. Fine (1998) studied the social world of amateur mushroom collectors, whose counterparts are professional mycologists. This is a thoroughgoing ethnography of the amateur side of the field of mycology. It adds greatly to our understand-ing of amateur science as shaped by the earlier studies of archaeologists and astronomers. In what is quite possibly the first study of adult figure skating as an amateur activity, McQuarrie and Jackson (1996) explored the constraints on a skater's progress through his or her serious leisure career in this activity. The authors found that, as they pass through the five stages of that career, adult amateur ice skaters encounter and often successfully negotiate a variety of constraints.

Career Volunteers

Although, today, volunteering is the most studied of the three types of serious leisure, it was the last of them to be defined by me and integrated into the Perspective. My first statement on volunteering appeared in Stebbins (1982a), which was subsequently elaborated in Stebbins (1996b). As for my empirical work on this type, I had observed their central role in helping maintain the Calgary French community (Stebbins, 1994b), but did not actually attempt a direct study of volunteers until somewhat later (Stebbins, 1998d). In the latter I described, for the first time, the role of key volunteers in sustaining organizations and communities, as this kind of civil labor generates a sense of self-fulfillment in such people (see chap. 1).

The real inaugural year for the study of career volunteering, however, was 1997. Six publications appeared that year, several of them appearing in a special issue of *World Leisure and Recreation* (v.39, n. 3, 1997). Works published that year, including those in that special issue, were written by Arai and Pedlar, Jarvis and King, Cuskelly and Harrington, and Thompson, who wrote both a doctoral dissertation and a journal article. They are summarized in Stebbins (2001a, pp. 117-119). Three years later a special issue bearing on the question of volunteering as leisure appeared in *Loisir et Société/Society and Leisure* (v. 23, n. 2, 2000). The contents of this issue and those of the book I edited with Margaret Graham (Stebbins and Graham, 2004) that bear directly on career volunteering are reviewed in chapter 2 of the present volume. Our object in the 2004 anthology was to assemble an international collection of studies on career volunteering.

It seems fair to conclude that research and theorizing on volunteering is, at present, the most dynamic wing of the serious leisure perspective. As this book goes to press, work is well underway on another special issue edited by Graham and Stebbins in *Voluntary Action* (due out in late 2006 or early 2007). This one bears on ethics and volunteering (note that not all papers published here will bear on the serious leisure perspective per se). Another imminent landmark is *A Dictionary of Nonprofit Terms and Concepts* (Smith, Stebbins, and Dover, 2006), which attempts by means of over 1,200 entries and accompanying cross-references to integrate leisure and its three forms of leisure with the huge variety of concepts germane to and practices found in the nonprofit sector.

Imported Concepts

The serious leisure perspective is now, as noted earlier, a formal grounded theory, the result of systematic exploration started in early 1974. Discussions of the nature of grounded theory give the impression that such constructions are created entirely and directly from data through the process of induction. Whereas it is possible, I should suppose, to develop a formal grounded theory by this (dare I say purest) approach, the present approach has also been constituted of several important imported concepts: concepts defined and elaborated outside the serious leisure perspective and brought into it to broaden its explanatory scope. I think it will be evident below how much these so-called foreign ideas have added to the Perspective.

Indeed the fifteen-year project began with several imported ideas, among them career, commitment, identity, and volunteer/volunteering. The aim of this section is to show how and where, over the course of the history of the Perspective, still other imported ideas have been brought in and what they have added to it by dint of their presence.

One of the more recent imports has already been introduced in this book (in chap. 1), namely, that of *social world*. Publication of Unruh's (1979; 1980) crisp elaboration of this idea (it had been discussed in more nebulous terms by earlier thinkers) enabled me to flesh out considerably the nature of the fifth distinctive quality of serious leisure: unique ethos. In this regard I drew on this idea for the first time, albeit in a rather superficial way, in the report on the Project (Stebbins, 1992a, p. 7). Social world became a main concept in the study of barbershop singers (Stebbins, 1996a) and the nature challenge hobbies (Stebbins, 2005c) as well as in the framework established for examining the organizational basis of leisure motivation (Stebbins, 2002).

Another imported concept is that of *lifestyle*. Veal (1993) did a great deal to bring this concept into leisure studies. My elaboration of it (Stebbins, 1997b) extended his thoughts into serious leisure, where it has served to anchor subsequent analyses of, for example, volunteers and the three mountain hobbies (Stebbins, 1998a; 2005c). The synthesizing concepts of optimal leisure lifestyle and discretionary time commitment sprang from this conceptual base (see chap. 4).

A third conceptual import is the idea of *central life interest* (Dubin, 1992). It was discussed in chapter 1 as an element in the uncontrollability of serious leisure. It first appeared in the literature on the Perspective in Stebbins (1992a, p. 3). To the extent that lifestyles form around complicated, absorbing, fulfilling activities, as they invariably do in serious leisure, these lifestyles can also be viewed as behavioral expressions of the participants' central life interests in those activities (Stebbins, 2001a, p. 20).

Social capital and *civil labor,* together, constitute a fourth imported concept, which has helped tie the serious leisure perspective to communitarian and societal levels of analysis. It was said in chapter 4 that, for the most part, civil labor is the contribution to community that amateurs, hobbyists, and career volunteers make when they pursue their serious leisure (Rojek, 2002, pp. 26-27). Furthermore civil labor, however conceived of, generates social capital. I have also used this same line of reasoning as a partial explanation of the ways social organization motivates leisure participation (see Stebbins. 2002, pp. 111-113).

Yet another imported idea is that of *deviance as leisure*. It entered the serious leisure perspective via two avenues: myself (Stebbins, 1997a) and Chris Rojek (1997). My textbook on deviance in Canada (Stebbins, 1996d) analyzed some of the several kinds of deviance using a general leisure framework, without specifying however, which kinds were casual and which were serious. The section on deviance in chapter 5 (of the present volume) establishes deviant leisure as a part of all leisure, while situating such leisure in the serious leisure perspective.

These five imported concepts have come from sociology. From the psychology of leisure I have taken the idea of *flow* (Csikszentmihalyi, 1990), which is part of the basic framework of serious leisure (chap. 1). I first related this concept to serious leisure in Stebbins (1992a, pp. 112, 127). Later I examined the experience of flow among barbershop singers (Stebbins, 1996a, pp. 67-68) and still later among kayakers, snowboarders, and mountain/ice climbers (Stebbins, 2005c, chap. 5).

Psychologists have also looked at leisure and *well-being* (e.g., Haworth, 1997). My first statement linking well-being and serious leisure was presented in Haworth's collection (Stebbins, 1997f, chap. 8), which is presented, with additional thoughts on the matter, in chapter 5 of the present book. It warrants repeating here the two basic propositions that emerged from that part of that chapter: (1) social well-being emanates from a high quality of life, as generated through the three forms of leisure and (2) self-fulfillment through leisure leads to well-being and on to mental and physical health.

Selfishness, which I described and conceptualized in general terms (Stebbins, 1981), has both psychological and sociological aspects. My initial statement on this attitude bore only incidentally on leisure, in that some of the examples given by my research subjects came from that part of their lives. Later (Stebbins, 1995b) I brought the idea into the serious leisure perspective, and then in chapter 1 of the present volume, I identified it as one of the consequences of uncontrollability as well as one of the issues of interest in the ethics of leisure behavior.

The importation of concepts could not always be done without significantly modifying them to fit better the world of leisure. I do not wish to go into detail here on this procedure, since I have already done so in other passages of this book. Suffice it to indicate briefly those concepts that have been substantially elaborated for this reason. They are lifestyle (chap. 4), career (chap. 1), professional (chap. 1), and volunteer/volunteering (chap. 1). Such modification is to be welcomed and encouraged in social scientific theory, for it broadens the scope of the ideas thus treated, while giving each a wider empirical base than heretofore.

Casual Leisure

Casual leisure, as already observed, got its start in the Perspective at the same time as serious leisure, but served only as a foil for the latter until I presented a separate conceptual statement on it in 1997 (Stebbins, 1997a). Central to that statement was the proposition that casual leisure is essentially hedonic. This claim sparked a good deal of debate, for the hedonic characterization was taken by some critics to mean that casual leisure had no merit. I attempted to set the record straight in a subsequent article (Stebbins, 2001b), in which I noted that, for all its hedonism, casual leisure did certainly generate a number of benefits. These have been described in chapter 3, along with still other benefits noted by Kleiber (2000) and Hutchinson and Kleiber (2005).

Nevertheless debate on the role of casual leisure waxed most intensely in the field of leisure education. It was sparked by my claim (Stebbins, 1999) that leisure education revolves around serious leisure (project-based leisure had not yet been conceptualized), a stance that then became part of a draft position paper on leisure education developed by the Educational Commission (EdComm) of the World Leisure & Recreation Association (today known as World Leisure). The draft stated that people of all ages should be informed of the differences separating serious and casual leisure, but after learning this, they should then be told about serious leisure, where it can be found, and what its benefits, costs, and rewards are.

The matter provoked an international discussion, with people weighing in from, among other countries, Australia, New Zealand, Great Britain, the Netherlands, Germany, Israel, and Canada and the United States. A discussion of the issues was organized at the First International Congress on Leisure Education held March 2004 in Cologne, Germany. Douglas Kleiber and I were among the keynote speakers on the opening evening of that event, by which point, I believe, he, I, and the others had largely ironed out our differences. As things stand today in leisure education circles, to the extent that people care to consider the issue, casual leisure is not generally seen as something we need to teach people how to do (with a few exceptions acknowledged such as relaxation), but that people still need to know that some of it can be mighty beneficial. The goal of leisure education is, therefore, to help people find a personally fulfilling *balance* in their leisure lifestyle, achieved by engaging in a combination of both forms, to which I now add the third form: project-based leisure.

As for EdComm's draft position paper, it was subsequently published, with rather little change, as an approved document written by Hillel Ruskin, chair of the commission, and Atara Sivan (Ruskin and Sivan, n.d., pp. 167-170).[1] This volume also contains a draft paper on casual leisure (pp. 171-173), which addresses the benefits of this form. These two papers, Ruskin's untimely death in 2004, the several clarifying statements made in the years leading up to the Congress, and perhaps general fatigue with the entire debate have brought silence on the matter.

Casual leisure's role as foil to serious leisure will very likely continue. When the general public thinks of leisure, it tends to have casual leisure in mind, suggesting that discussions with the public about serious leisure cannot escape comparing the two forms. In other words casual leisure offers a recognizable backdrop, which facilitates understanding of serious leisure and, for that matter, of project-based leisure. The important message to emerge from the ferment that preceded the 2004 Congress is that casual leisure, no matter how hedonic, is not trivial. Its benefits, many of which, I am sure, remain to be discovered, should be recognized and communicated, along with, of course, the benefits and rewards of the other two forms.

Project-Based Leisure

Being the newcomer that it is (first publication on it by Stebbins, 2005a), project-based leisure still has no significant history to report on. But it is in keeping with the present chapter to describe the circumstances that gave rise to the idea. The "discovery" of project-based leisure was pure serendipity, an anomaly, perhaps, in a field so rooted in exploratory research as the serious leisure perspective is.

Serendipity is the quintessential form of informal experimentation, accidental discovery, and spontaneous invention. It contrasts sharply with exploration, described earlier as a broad-ranging, purposive, systematic, prearranged undertaking (Stebbins, 2001c, pp. 3-4). It turned out to be a serendipitous evening for me, as I attended a surprise sixtieth birthday party for a close friend. Peggy's sixtieth birthday was three months off, when three members of her immediate family decided to stage a surprise party to celebrate the occasion in grand style. A division of labor was struck, in which father would book a restaurant and invite the guests, while the son and one of the daughters would assemble a detailed slide show of Peggy's life, running from her birth to the present. With twenty-five guests and the need to invite them secretly, father was undertaking some project-based leisure of his own (best classified here as informal volunteering). Nonetheless, the project of his two children was even more complicated and time consuming, and for these reasons, is the one on which we will concentrate here.

To build their slide show (a project in entertainment theatre), they had to contact maternal relatives in distant parts of the country to obtain copies of earlier photographs of Peggy and of important people and events in her life. This material was then assembled into a chronological account of her main work and leisure activities up to her sixtieth year. Some specialized background knowledge was required to create the slide show, for it was to be projected by computer. So it fell to Peggy's son to attend to this facet of the project, while her daughter saw to rounding up the photographs and developing a story line.

The show consisted of 180 slides, which were presented in a forty-five-minute session following the dinner. Peggy, from whom the entire event had been successfully kept secret, was flabbergasted by it all. Enormously pleased with everything that had occurred that evening, she found it hard to fathom the amount of effort that her son and daughter had put into the slide project and how well it turned out.

The rewards experienced by the son and daughter included self-actualization (e.g., learned a great deal about extended family), self-expression (e.g., computer skills), and self-image among the twenty-five guests as producers of the "fantastic" slide show. The son and daughter experienced the reward of group accomplishment as well as, since their project also required collaboration with others. Moreover, since both held full-time jobs, it is quite possible that their project further served as temporary re-creation.

As I sat through the various phases of the evening's celebration, my mind wondered, as it often does, to the sphere of my professional interest, notably, leisure. What kind of leisure was this? It was clearly not serious leisure, one reason being that there was no career in so short an undertaking. At the same time it was far more complex than typical casual leisure. In fact, some past skills and knowledge were brought into play (e.g., computer skills), while other aspects of the project required only routine phoning and mailing (of invitations). Before I left the party that evening, I had concluded that this was a project, and that, in leisure, projects like this one are sufficiently different from the casual and serious forms to warrant their own classificatory home.

In the development of the serious leisure perspective, this serendipitous discovery was, obviously, a highly important step. All leisure could no longer be classified according to whether it is serious or casual. This having been said, the challenge today, just as it was when serious leisure was first broached in the 1970s, is to get to work on a set of exploratory studies that empirically anchor project-based leisure and, using the grounded data they will generate, to check the validity of the ideas contained in the conceptual statement of 2005 and, of course, to add new concepts and propositions to it.

Conclusions

This has been a history of the serious leisure perspective. The historical background of the Perspective is as important, and important for the same reasons, as historical background is for each kind of leisure studied (see chap. 4). We very much need to see how events, social arrangements, and culture combine to shape the emergence and development of scientific frameworks. Put otherwise we need for each kind of leisure, where it is feasible, a contextual analysis leading to a sociology of knowledge of that activity.

But when we speak of history we invariably raise the question of the future of the subject of that history. Historians are fond of pointing out that the "past is prologue." The final chapter of this book centers on the future of the serious leisure perspective, which I think (no bias here, of course) is bright.

Note

1.   The omission of a date of publication is unfortunate. Given the dates of some of the references in the text, I suspect that the book was released in 2002 or 2003.

7

Importance of the Perspective

In chapter 5 I concentrated on placing the serious leisure perspective in interdisciplinary context. Now we must go still farther a field to determine how the perspective fits globally, how it fits in this world in the present epoch. In this final chapter I take up, first, the question of why it is necessary to classify leisure activities. I then address myself to how the Perspective applies outside the West, and thus to the question of what it can offer to the world as a whole. Next comes a discussion of the relationship of the serious leisure perspective to health and well-being. The chapter then moves on to look at leisure and its place in the nonprofit sector. In the Conclusion I underscore the importance of finding balance among the three forms of the Perspective, of finding an optimal leisure lifestyle, and of using leisure education to achieve these goals.

Classifying Leisure

In the most fundamental, scientific sense, classification of a particular phenomenon being studied study needs no defense. All sciences categorize the things they investigate, if for no other reason, than to render research there more manageable through generalization. In the mammalian classification system found in biology, categorizing animals by whether they are, for instance, ungulates or carnivores is more efficient than dealing separately with, for example, deer, moose, and buffalo (ungulates) or wolves, foxes, and coyotes (carnivores). This approach is more efficient because researchers can generalize about properties and processes common to all ungulates or carnivores. Of course, such generalizations sometimes obscure an important quality of an individual member of the classification, which must then be examined separately.

David Smith (2000, pp. 232-233) distinguished between "purposive" and "analytic," or "theoretic," classifications of voluntary groups. The first are superficial and highly descriptive, based on some obvious characteristic shared by a set of groups. Awhile back I constructed for my book on leisure for people without work a purposive, seventeen-class, typology of volunteering (Stebbins, 1998a, pp. 74-80). It included such types as volunteering in education, the provision of necessities, civic affairs, health, and the physical environment, which enabled me to describe the scope of volunteering as a type of leisure activity (as found in any of the three forms).

Theoretic classifications are different, however. They are based on concepts or data from research or, ideally, both. Consequently they are subject to empirical validation, which is to say that, in light of new data suggesting that we modify them, we are forced to act accordingly. At least we *should* act accordingly, to avoid the charge made by Samdahl (1999, p. 124) that "typologies have an air of formality and finality that can too easily be taken for reality." A rare example of theoretic classification in leisure studies is provided by Gunter and Gunter (1980), who classified leisure lifestyles according to whether they are pure leisure, anomic leisure, organized leisure, or alienated leisure. They considered leisure activities along two dimensions: (a) time/choice/structure and type and (b) degree of psychological involvement in a particular activity. By cross-classifying these two dimensions, they generated these four types. Other theoretic classifications of leisure include those of Kelly on lifestyle (1999, pp. 145-147), Mannell on leisure satisfaction (1999, p. 239), Crawford and Godbey on constraints (1987), and Rojek on the class basis of deviant leisure (1999, pp. 88-90).

It is also noteworthy that leisure studies abounds with twofold typologies. Sometimes interest here revolves around one type, with the other being used as a foil. As observed earlier the study of serious leisure began this way, taking casual leisure as its comparative backdrop. Likewise distinctions have been drawn between mass and elite leisure, active and sedentary leisure, men's leisure and that of women, and so on. And, from the beginning of thought about leisure, there has been a tendency to contrast it with work. Aristotle said that finding time for leisurely contemplation is a main goal of work; that the reason for working is to sustain life, thus leaving us time for contemplation.

But all these theoretic classifications center on a particular aspect of leisure: lifestyle, satisfaction, constraints, level of activity, social-class basis of the activity. Meanwhile classifications bearing on whole of leisure, which are uncommon, have been purposive. Consider, for example, Kaplan's (1975, chap. 13) social systemic typology, which categorized all leisure as physical, intellectual, artistic, sociable, or practical. An earlier classification developed by Havighurst and Feigenbaum (1959) contained eleven descriptive types, among them, play, participation in organized groups, participation in sport, spectator sports, and fishing and hunting.

The three forms and their types and subtypes as served up in the serious leisure perspective constitute a theoretic typology of leisure, which as near as I can tell, now embraces the whole of leisure. I believe the preceding chapters have shown, in sufficient variety of ways, how this typology is rooted in both theory and data. In this respect it differs from the typologies of Kaplan and Havighurst and Feigenbaum. Note, further, that there is better than a thirty-year gap between their work and publication of this book, and that there has been little interest during this period in developing a theoretic classification system designed to cover all leisure. I, too, am implicated in this indictment, for I was not, at the time, self-consciously pursuing such a goal.

Lack of such a typology also points to lack of an all-embracing theory of leisure. This is not, however, to argue that there is, in leisure studies, an absence of theory. Quite the contrary, Rojek's (2005) *tour d'horizon* of this field shows just how rich it is in theory, while I have, in a related way, shown the same for leisure concepts (Stebbins, 2005f). The serious leisure perspective does not even begin to incorporate all the theories covered by Rojek, though it does incorporate some of them while linking into several others. Moreover no one may claim that the serious leisure perspective summarizes all leisure theory. Rather what it does accomplish is narrower, even if it still presents a broad picture of the field: it offers a classification and explanation of all leisure (core) activity and experience, with attention also given to the associated social, cultural, and historical contexts in which the activity and experience take place.

The serious leisure perspective stands apart from the aforementioned theoretic and purposive types in its substantial rootedness in the routine life of *homo otiosus*. Most people in society do not go about their routine leisure thinking of it as mass, elite, alienated, anomic, sedentary, or even playful. The respondents in my research did, however, have a sense of being amateur, hobbyist, or volunteer; these were concepts they knew. They recognized, too, that they were amateur musicians, hobbyist barbershop singers, and volunteer members of a school committee. And they recognized casual leisure, contrasting it with what they did as "serious" leisure. Finally, though we need research to formally validate this claim, my informal observations suggest that people also know when they are involved in project-based leisure. In short, many concepts in the basic statements of the three forms presented in chapters 1 and 3 have much the same meaning for leisure participants as for scholars who study them.

This has been the singular advantage of using exploratory methodology and grounded theory construction to establish the conceptual and theoretic foundation of this Perspective. It is also the approach to follow, if we want to avoid Samdahl's aforementioned critique of leisure typologies. That is we must *always* explore—even when the field of research has reached the confirmatory stage—to ascertain how old activities and experiences have changed as well as to discover and explore the new ones that have recently been created (Stebbins, 2001c, p. 9).

The Modern Proliferation of Leisure Activities

Typologies simplify and organize an undifferentiated mass of phenomena found to have one or more features in common, in the case of leisure, the Perspective has simplified and organized an undifferentiated mass of free-time core activities and experiences. Today that mass of activities and experiences seems to be growing, almost exponentially. I have never encountered an explanation for this trend, but one observation is clear, we in leisure studies would be foolish to ignore it. And what better way to recognize the new activities and experiences and simultaneously test out the comprehensiveness of the serious leisure perspective than to ask how and where the former fit within the latter. I illustrate below with three.

In the absence of proper exploratory, field research, let us speculate a bit. New to your author, though not, it appears, in Tunisia, is the Tunisian game of Oggaf, or sand hockey. It is played with sticks made from branches of nearby palm trees and a ball fashioned from dromedary hair. Exploratory study of the game might reveal its hobbyist nature, or were the six distinguishing qualities missing, its status as casual leisure. The picture of the game I saw in the 29 December 2005 issue of the *Calgary Herald* (p. A22), was of it being played during the 36th Sahara Festival in Douz, Tunisia. It is possible that it is only played at that time, making it, conceivably, a kind of project-based leisure.

Let us turn to our second illustration. The community in which I live has recently taken to organizing "conversation cafés." These casual leisure, sociable conversations operate fortnightly on a no-charge basis, and are held in a public setting, usually a local café. Anyone may participate, which is done by speaking in turn on a mutually-agreed-upon subject. This session is followed by open dialogue. A skilled host leads the session, and people who would rather not to speak may simply listen or participant only in the subsequent dialogue. Although not a form of civil labor, conversation cafés do seem to generate a certain amount of social capital.

For my third example I turn, again, to the field of hobbies, this time the subtype of making and tinkering. Tompkins (2003) writes on the activities of hobbyist builders of flight decks, people (usually men, it appears) who construct a mock airplane cockpit in their garage or basement or, believe it or not, their bedroom. Equipped electronically, much like the modern airplane, these flight decks get used as flight simulators, allowing their operators to "fly" in different kinds of weather, at various altitudes, at a number of speeds, and so on. Equipment for these constructions is not cheap, however, making this hobby one for the wealthy.

As indicated these three taxonomic placements are speculative. To do the job properly, would require open-ended, ethnographic examination of each activity. New activities must first be assessed for their fit with the six distinguishing qualities to determine if they are serious, casual, or project-based leisure. Admittedly, this is time consuming, but should we fail to explore well the new activities, we risk misclassifying them and, worse, we may miss discovering a new form. (The advantages of SLIM—the serious leisure scale discussed in chap. 2—are evident here.) Remember: the serious leisure perspective and its three forms are founded on what we know. And what we do not know, but can discover, may show that the Perspective or its forms need modification (of certain generalizations, of the number of forms, of certain synthesizing links, etc.).

The Serious Leisure Perspective Globalized

Oggaf was tentatively classified as serious leisure. Indeed the serious leisure perspective is now reasonably international, that is, it has generated research or guided application in, among other countries and regions, Great Britain, the Netherlands, Belgium, Spain, Portugal, Israel, Brazil, Australia, New Zealand, and North America. Reference has been made at various points in this book to work in these places. So we may say that the Perspective is international, but it is nonetheless largely Western. In the Perspective the developing world is conspicuous by its absence.

Of course, leisure studies, in general, is weak outside the West and a few of the former Communist-bloc countries. But this situation is no excuse for failing to come to grips with this huge gap in knowledge. The issue of serious leisure outside the First World stands apart from other issues in leisure in that, to my knowledge, it has never been raised in the literature, that is, it has not yet emerged as a matter of debate among researchers (I do discuss it in Stebbins, 2001a, pp. 132-134). But it certainly has stirred comment among students, notably those in the international masters program of the World Leisure and Recreation Centre of Excellence (WICE), where I have taught from time to time since its inception in 1992. Their views of the role, frequency, and dispersion of serious leisure in their countries have been illuminating.

The greatest contrasts exist between the first and third worlds. Students from Asia, Africa, and Latin America, for example, believe that, compared with the West, serious leisure is much rarer in their countries, and some forms of it hardly seem to exist there at all. They acknowledge the practice of amateur sport, but not that of amateur science. Amateur art and entertainment are vague ideas for them, since both fields merge with their folkloristic counterparts. Collecting, as serious leisure, is largely a foreign interest to them, as are the liberal arts hobbies and nearly all the activities classified as activity participation (hunting, fishing, and the folk arts being exceptions). More familiar is the hobby of making things, particularly baskets and clothing as well as making pottery and raising animals. But with the making and participation activities that they do know, there is, in a way similar to the arts and entertainment fields, a blurring of the line separating what is obligatory from what is nonobligatory leisure. The concept of competitive sports, games, and contests is familiar, but the activities themselves, which are so common in the first world, are much less so outside it. Some students speak of amateur and hobbyist serious leisure, in general, as being available only to their country's elite, whose leisure tastes, the students believe, have been influenced by the West.

Students from the third world do recognize the act of volunteering, but hold that much of it is enacted differently there. Organizational volunteering is much less common than the grass roots type, while informal volunteering—helping—appears to be considerably more widespread than either of the two formal kinds. Even here, in ways largely unknown in the first world, the line separating obligation and voluntary action is fuzzy. For example, in some countries, the expectation of helping is institutionalized, as seen in the practice found in parts of Columbia where every man in the village is obligated to help when one of them builds a house. Invoking the serious leisure perspective, we would ask whether the obligation is felt as agreeable.

Students from the second world countries (those of the former Communist bloc), seem to look on serious leisure in much the same way as those from the first world. Nevertheless, the milieu in which it is pursued is dramatically different, given the vast social, economic, and cultural adjustments that have been taking place since the Communist system started formally unravelling in the latter half of the 1980s. In other words, in this part of the globe, participation in serious leisure is as much in flux as participation in the rest of life. Given the scope, subtlety, and evanescence of these adjustments, students from these countries have found it difficult to identify their effects on serious leisure there. Jung offers a good description of the present situation in Poland, thereby suggesting what it may be like in other second world countries:

> While the context presented above seeks to offset the unidimensional optimism flowing from quantitative analysis of leisure statistics, it perhaps needs to be reappraised in the context of increased personal freedom, unprecedented choice, individualization of life patterns and opportunities offered by the "new times," but available to those who have the means, skills and interest to take advantage of them. Activities which were very time consuming under Communism's widespread shortages. . .disappeared, but they were replaced by the need to take additional jobs to meet newly created wants and, more often, simply to make ends meet (Jung, 2005, p. 218).

He also comments on the tendency to participate less in the collective and socialized forms of leisure and more in those based at home or in privatized facilities. Furthermore, this trend is nurturing the growth of individualized leisure, which hints at a possible upswing in the pursuit of the predominantly self-interested forms of serious leisure, the hobbies and amateur activities.

The lesson in all this is clear: research and theorizing in serious leisure, which has so far has come almost exclusively from the First World, is by no means always generalizable to countries outside it. The WICE students have identified some of the areas where we must exercise caution. Still, volunteering of some sort serves as a common leisure ground among these students, and Henderson and Presley (2003) argue, across the world. Volunteering (both casual and career), the authors hold, can bring people together everywhere, whether in local villages or on a global scale. Personal interests may be pursued via this avenue, but it can also foster communitarian and global commitments creating, in the process, human capital.

Non-Western Leisure

How might we go about identifying non-Western leisure? First, it is reasonable to assume that, in every society, most members enjoy a certain amount of free time and that they pursue some sort of leisure within this period of their lives. This is the dominant pattern, which in some societies, contrasts with another pattern: the lack of this kind of time among some people (e.g., the harried, all-work-and-no-play drudge found in some

Western societies). I believe this assumption about the universality of free time holds, even though opportunities for sport, leisure and tourism are, compared with the West, substantially less prevalent in developing countries (Sheykhi, 2003).

Second, the sort of leisure pursued will often differ substantially from that pursued in the West, though in this regard, globalization may now be generating a certain level of international homogeneity. Consequently someone intending to study leisure in a third world country would do well to try to find out, first-hand, what the locals define as free time and leisure, as opposed to arriving with a list of leisure activities known to be pursued in the West. Matejko (1984) discusses some of the problems that come with taking the latter approach.

But how does a researcher go about discovering what leisure is in local terms, when it is likely that local people have no concept of free time or of the leisure nature of activities undertaken within it? I suggest the following steps:

First look for three types of activities:

1. Those people like to do and do not have to do;
2. Those people like to do and also have to do; and
3. Those people do not like to do, but must do them anyway.

A combination of participant observation and informal question asking should, in most instances, provide answers to these three questions. Answers to 1 and 2 would qualify as leisure in Western terms (see in chap. 1 the definition of leisure as uncoerced activity that people want to do). Free time may be inferred from time left over after people have met the obligations implied in 3. Although it might be difficult to determine whether those disagreeable obligations were fulfilled as part of work or as part of something required outside work, this for the student of leisure, would matter little. For this person the third type of activity is of peripheral concern relative to the first two.

But, you might argue, why not also regard type 2 as peripheral? After all it, too, is obligatory. To do this would leave a clean division between type 1, which for some scholars is the proper focus of leisure studies, and types 2 and 3. This conceptual maneuver could expose the researcher to the charge of Western bias, however, for as I have observed elsewhere (Stebbins, 2004b), finding work in the West that is so attractive that it is essentially experienced as leisure (i.e., type 2 activity) is not a commonly achieved goal. Moreover, most Westerners do not even expect to find such "devotee" work. And so it is in the West. Meanwhile we should never assume that the rest of the world qualifies some or all of its work in the same terms.

Then there is the matter of obligation. I argued earlier that a person can find pleasant, agreeable obligations in certain activities, in this way further validating type 2 as a legitimate concern for leisure researchers working anywhere, including the third world. An example from the West might be the leading lady who is obligated to go to the theatre during the weekend to perform in an amateur play, but does so with great enthusiasm rooted in her passion for drama as leisure activity. By contrast, her obligation to turn up at work the following Monday morning after the deep satisfaction of the preceding leisure weekend comes as a letdown. An example from an African country might be the sense of fulfilment gained from skilfully, knowledgeably, and creatively decorating a clay pot. The pot is needed for water, whereas its decoration, rather than being utilitarian, becomes an occasion for hobbyist artistic expression.

The foregoing example of the sport of Oggaf is, depending on the conditions of play, non-Western serious or project-based leisure. Moreover, casual leisure has been observed outside the West, though it was not interpreted as such. Be that as it may Yedes, Clamons, and Osman (2004) write about the practice of "buna" in Ethiopia. In buna Muslim Oromo women gather over coffee, where, among other activities, they share stories, communicate with Allah, show support for one another as well as promote familial and communitarian harmony.

Global Import of the Perspective

Researchers and theorists in the West have been at work for some time on aspects of the serious leisure perspective, the list in the preceding section showing the international scope of this effort. That scope is largely Western, nevertheless, and it is, for the most part, purely scientific, in the sense that the Perspective has not widely influenced practice. Still, I mentioned earlier some instances of application of the Perspective that, together, suggest ways it can make an impact on society well beyond the academy. I will review them briefly here.

In chapter 5 we considered the adoption in Israel of a leisure education program for primary and secondary schools, wherein both serious and casual leisure are centerpieces. This is one instance of application. Another was mentioned in chapter 2. It is the training project mounted by Bramante (2004) in Sorocaba, Brazil, which he designed to stimulate civil labor among youth and enable them to contribute to their country's social capital. Youth were trained to engage in career volunteering, as both a personal and a communitarian benefit.

The third instance, which has not yet been covered in this book, is the report of the Hillary Commission on Sport, Fitness, and Leisure in New Zealand. The Commission was established in 1987 under a mandate from the Government of New Zealand to develop and encourage sport and active living for all.[1] It had two goals: one was to increase participation in sport, fitness, and leisure, the other was to achieve high levels of success in international sporting competition. It is not my purpose here to review the successes and failures of the Commission, this having been carried out in detail by Pringle (2001). The point to be made in this chapter is that serious and casual leisure were among the conceptual tools used by the Commission in analyzing the sport, fitness, and leisure situation in New Zealand and in making recommendations based on their findings.

Turning to the field of retirement policy, Kelly (1997, p. 177) has proposed that retirees be encouraged to try to "direct their lives in a balance of engagement that is at least relatively satisfying." I pointed out in an earlier chapter that this assumes adequate health, income, companionship, and transportation. It also assumes that the elderly know there are leisure activities that can be seriously pursued, which brings us once again to the crucial role of leisure education in promulgating the serious leisure perspective.

There has also been a move into policy in the area of adult education and self-directed learning. It was noted in chapter 5 that Jones and Symon (2001), in writing about governmental policy in Britain, indicate that these two offer serious learning-oriented resources for six special groups: the unemployed, unwaged (volunteers), elderly, women, "portfolio workers" (hold many different jobs over a lifetime), and people with disabilities. Moreover serious leisure offers an involving, fulfilling career to these groups that some members of them once had and other members of them never had in work. Contemporary governmental policy, the authors say, tends to overlook the existence of serious leisure and its implications for quality of life and well-being.

Patterson has continued to extend serious leisure into the field of disabilities studies and practice. For instance he has recommended that community-based agencies serving people with disabilities implement leisure counselling and educational services as well as hire trained leisure counsellors to support their clients (Patterson, 2000). Given the subsequent addition of project-based leisure to the Perspective, I now add that form of leisure to this exhortation. In a later paper Patterson

(2001) argues that we should center our leisure education programs for the intellectually disabled on serious leisure activities. Such activities can engender self-respect, self-esteem, and lead to greater acceptance and social inclusion in the larger community. Aitchison (2003, p. 956) adds for people with disabilities in general that pursuing serious leisure may enhance physical health and fitness as well as reduce risk of illness. For the reason just given, we can also add project-based leisure to this recommendation for programs in leisure education.

Jenna Hartel has pioneered the extension of serious leisure into leisure information science (LIS), a field oriented as much toward application of research as toward generating new data. Hartel (2003) points out that, historically, LIS has heavily favored the study of scholarly and professional informational domains, while largely ignoring those related to leisure. In a move to help redress this imbalance, she introduces the study of information in hobbies. Serious leisure is examined for its library and informational forces and properties as these relate to a particular core leisure activity and the organizational milieu in which it is pursued. Clearly the patterns of storage, retrieval, and dissemination will vary considerably from one core activity to another. Hartel is currently conducting research on the hobby of cooking.

Arts administration is dominantly an applied field of knowledge, so that my own work here (Stebbins, 2005e) constitutes still another direct link to policy. As observed in chapter 5 most people who attend arts events (e.g., concerts, festivals, performances, exhibitions) or patronize arts facilities (e.g., galleries, museums, libraries) are seeking a leisure experience. Thus of use to arts administrators, whose job is, in part, to market the arts they have been hired to manage, is knowledge about this experience, particularly knowledge about its nature and its distribution in the population of potential arts buffs and consumers.

Finally, informal discussions with colleagues in the field of tourism management reveal that some of them see the importance of serious and casual leisure as a way of explaining the appeal of the several varieties of cultural tourism. For example, these two forms help explain why people are attracted to special events such as the Edinburgh Fringe Festival, the Montreux Jazz Festival, and the Calgary Stampede and Exhibition. The entire serious leisure perspective can help explain the attraction of adventure tourism and, as noted earlier, volunteer tourism. Special interest tourism, as seen in wine and architecture tours, can likewise be understood using the serious leisure perspective.

Leisure and Health

I hinted late in chapter 5 at the link between leisure and health. I now want to flesh out my thesis.

I get the impression that, in health circles, the term "leisure" is a dirty word. At least this sphere of life only seems to be discussed there in pejorative terms, I suspect because it is regarded, not as an avenue to the Heaven of good health, but as a road to the Hell of bad health. This commonsense view of the place of leisure in everyday life is, to be sure, partly valid. Some people do smoke, drink (alcohol), and eat too much, live a sedentary existence in their free time, and watch television to the point of dulling their wits, all done in the name of leisure. Boredom in free time, though technically not leisure, as was pointed out earlier, is nevertheless a further popular indicator of the (mentally) unhealthy lifestyle that can develop after work and other obligations are finished.

But, as stated in chapter 5, leisure can also bring healthy benefits. In that chapter I observed that, although the relationship is probably more complex than this, we may say, in general terms, that self-fulfillment, whether achieved through serious or project-based leisure or devotee work, leads to enhanced quality of life and well-being, and then, on to improved psychological health and physical health, to the extent the second is influenced by the first. So the road to the Hell of bad health may be paved with too steady a diet of casual leisure, but the one leading to the Heaven of good health is paved with a judicious amount of serious leisure, and we must now add in light of the serious leisure perspective, mixed with some casual or project-based leisure, if not both. In other words to find an optimal leisure lifestyle is to get on the road to good health.

All this, however, is best understood within the framework of preventive medicine. Obviously, if a person already has bad or weak physical health, an optimal leisure lifestyle is not, in itself, going to miraculously restore him to a healthy state. Conceivably, for example, someone with, say, bone cancer could still develop an optimal leisure lifestyle, which might in some positive way affect future mental health. In the meantime, however, that person is physically unhealthy and, so far as we know, leisure can do nothing to ameliorate the cancer. So the fulfillment $\rightarrow$ quality of life $\rightarrow$ well-being $\rightarrow$ health proposition is most applicable in the preventive sphere of health.

Unfortunately preventive medicine, as a profession, seems largely unaware of this proposition. In January, 2005, I presented a seminar on it to the professors and graduate students of the newly established Markin Institute at the University of Calgary. The Institute's mandate is to conduct research on and improve practice in preventive medicine and public health. My talk appeared to be warmly received, in good part, I believe, because my ideas were seen as fresh. Few, if any, of those in attendance had thought of leisure as an avenue to the Heaven of good health, though it was clear that they knew of leisure's other road.

My little seminar has not transformed thinking in preventive medicine (even in Calgary, as far as I know), nor did I expect it would.[2] Here, as elsewhere in so much of modern life, the notion of leisure as a trivial pursuit dominates. Here, as elsewhere, there is, consequently, great need for leisure education.

Leisure and the Nonprofit Sector

The presentation in chapter 1 of volunteering as one of the three types of serious leisure hints at the key role leisure plays in the nonprofit sector of society. The following three definitions, taken from *A dictionary of nonprofit terms and concepts* (Smith, Stebbins, and Dover, 2006), show the nature and extent of this role.

- *Nonprofit sector*: generally put, the nonprofit sector encompasses all aspects of all nonprofit groups in a society, in addition to all individual voluntary action found there.
- *Nonprofit group*: a formal or informal group of people joined together to pursue a common not-for-profit goal. That is, it is not the intention of the group to distribute excess revenue to members or leaders or to operate mainly according to personal attachment as to a household or family. Nor is a nonprofit group a government agency.
- *Individual voluntary action*: voluntary action performed by an individual. In addition to activity by the individual in formal nonprofit groups, this concept includes certain activity in informal group and nongroup contexts motivated by voluntary altruism. Examples include informal service volunteering, informal economic support activity, informal interpersonal activity, informal political participation, informal religious activity, informal social innovation activity, and informal social esthetics activity.

Nearly all that is stated in these definitions as denoting the nonprofit sector may also be applied to a far amount of leisure. In fact the only areas of leisure that are not also part of the nonprofit world are household/family leisure and leisure containing no voluntary altruism. Though much of modern leisure can be considered part of the nonprofit sector, free-time activities not motivated by voluntary altruism, including most individual hedonic leisure (e.g., napping, strolling, daydreaming), lie outside that sector. According to Smith (2000, pp.19-20) altruism is voluntary when there is (1) a mix of humane caring and sharing of oneself and one's resources; (2) at least a moderate freedom to chose the activity; (3) a lack of coercion from biophysical, biosocial, or socially compelling forces; (4) a sensitivity to certain needs and wants of a target of benefits; (5) an expectation of little or no remuneration or payment in kind; and (6) an expectation of receiving some sort of satisfaction for action undertaken on behalf of the target. Smith's definition of voluntary altruism reads, in many ways, like our definition of leisure set out early in chapter 1.

Viewed from the angle of the serious leisure perspective, we may say that the nonprofit sector, on the one hand, and serious and project-based leisure, on the other, cover much the same ground, while casual leisure is, for the most part, found outside their territory. The critical question is whether voluntary altruism is possible when pursuing the core activity in question and whether the participant pursues it in an altruistic way. Thus, a piano player plays outside the nonprofit sector when doing so strictly for personal enjoyment and within that sector when forming part of a jazz ensemble. In the latter situation the musician shares his or her resources, shows sensitivity to the needs and wants of others in the group, while also meeting the remaining four criteria just listed by Smith. The same reasoning holds for the liberal arts hobbyist who reads solely for personal pleasure vis-à-vis someone who reads so that person can participate weekly in discussions at a book club. Similar examples can be found in project-based leisure, where a person might make a stereo tuner for self or for a friend or a charitable group, take a trip alone or with a friend (satisfaction with the trip depends, in part, on the friend's participation), or climb Mount Kilimanjaro alone or with a friend.

The import of all this lies in the new understanding gained from seeing the nonprofit sector in leisure terms. In chapter 1 we considered the volitional conception of volunteering as revolving, in significant part, around a central subjective motivational question: it must be determined whether volunteers feel they are engaging in an enjoyable (casual leisure), fulfilling (serious leisure), or enjoyable or fulfilling (project-based leisure) core activity that they have had the option to accept or reject on their own terms. Nevertheless the reigning conception of volunteering in nonprofit sector research is not this volitional one of volunteering as leisure, but another one: volunteering as unpaid work. This economic conception defines volunteering as the absence of payment as livelihood, whether in money or in kind. It largely avoids the messy question of motivation so crucial to the leisure conception, but does so at great cost. That cost is, no less, the failure to explain volunteering. The economic conception merely describes behavior in the nonprofit sector. It offers no explanation of that behavior; its fails to tell us why people engage in all sorts of leisure activities for no pay.

Conclusions

It is time to close this exposition of the serious leisure perspective, which I have chosen to do by way of metaphor. The metaphor is the famous New Orleans dessert: "Bananas Foster." And, if you wish, you may regard it as the final course of the meal you have consumed in reading this book.

Let us think, for a moment, of the serious leisure perspective as resembling a serving of Bananas Foster. Serious leisure is the central ingredient in this confection, which however, is greatly enhanced with the complementary ingredients of rum, salt butter, cinnamon, brown sugar, banana liqueur, and vanilla ice cream. They are, metaphorically speaking, casual and project-based leisure. All this is prepared to perfection in a flambé pan, where the rum serves as fuel for the fire that cooks the bananas, themselves bathed, as they are, in a sauce prepared from the aforementioned ingredients.

In metaphor or in real life, the bananas alone (serious leisure) are insufficient to constitute this dessert. Rather it needs for its completion and perfection the other ingredients, or metaphorically, casual or project-based leisure, if not both. The blending of the ingredients into a sauce and then cooking the bananas in it may be likened to searching, perhaps with the help of leisure education, for an optimal leisure lifestyle. Such a lifestyle is Bananas Foster, exquisitely prepared. Serious leisure is enhanced and blended with judicious amounts of appealing (dare I say, appetizing) casual or project-based leisure.

To continue the analogy, note that Bananas Foster is reasonably accessible to many people; the bananas, the ingredients, and even the flambé pan (may be substituted with a large heavy skillet) are available at modest cost. It is a popular dessert in New Orleans, in part because so many people can afford to prepare it. It is likewise with serious leisure and its accompaniments of casual and project-based leisure. All three forms subsume many free or low-priced activities that can be combined into an optimal leisure lifestyle.

Yet, there are people, perhaps most of them living in the West, who care little for Bananas Foster or simply have no time to eat it.[3] These people, once finished with everyday work and nonwork obligations, carve out a leisure lifestyle consisting of casual and possibly some project-based leisure. And there are, as shown in chapter 3, a number of benefits and rewards to come from these two, whether alone or in combination (i.e., in our metaphor, the sauce). These benefits and rewards should never be minimized, even if, as a dessert, they constitute a blander offering than Bananas Foster. But what gives the latter its special appeal is its potential for self-fulfillment (as it were, the bananas), which is missing altogether or substantially diluted in the other two forms. This omission is critical, for in leisure, in work, indeed, in life as a whole, I believe this book has shown that this fulfillment stands out as a very special personal state. The search for fulfillment in leisure is complex, and it motivates people in powerful ways.

But, alas, by no means everyone in the world—especially, it was previously observed, people outside the West—knows about Bananas Foster. It is not even on their menu. Correspondingly not everyone knows about the serious leisure perspective and about its personal manifestation as an optimal leisure lifestyle. Furthermore—and here, as often happens with metaphors, this one breaks down—many people are unaware of the principal ingredient of the serious leisure perspective, serious leisure itself (unlike bananas, which most everyone does know of). When asked what proportion of the population pursues serious leisure, I have often responded with the figure of, on average, about 20 percent of the overall population is involved in serious leisure of some kind. True, more than 20 percent may know about such leisure, but I estimate—and it is admittedly a crude estimate—that about this proportion actually pursues it. You may remember earlier mention of Polson's attempt to estimate the rate of serious leisure in the population. Though his basis for estimation appears to be no more solid than mine, he also comes to much the same conclusion about the distribution of serious leisure in the general population. He estimates this to be 15 to 25 percent (see his website, Polson, 2006)

Herein, then, we find the pivotal role of leisure education in this century (Cohen-Gewerc and Stebbins, in press). Given this present distribution of people who go in for the three forms of leisure, many more of them the world over could benefit from being aware of the serious leisure perspective, of its three forms, and of their interrelationship. Leisure education can help immensely in this regard. The optimal leisure lifestyle that can be fashioned from knowledge gained through such education, from knowing the Perspective, and taking action to realize a fulfilling optimal lifestyle available through it is the Bananas Foster of our routine existence.

In this special and subtle sense, the concept of serious leisure found in the label "serious leisure perspective" does communicate a bias. You may remember that, in the first paragraph of chapter 1, I maintained the opposite. And I stand by that claim, in that, by pursuing two or all three forms of the Perspective, we can achieve a leisure balance and fashion our own an optimal leisure lifestyle. But self-fulfillment is the quintessential element in this lifestyle, which tips the balance toward serious leisure pursued in some combination with casual or project-based leisure, or both. They, too, are essential ingredients in the dessert. But, then, Bananas Foster, *sans bananes*, is just not Bananas Foster. Every New Orleanian knows that.

Notes

1. In 2002 the Hillary Commission was joined with another governmental unit, the two together being renamed Sport and Recreation New Zealand (SPARC).
2. As I was putting the finishing touches on this manuscript, a draft plan for the Markin Institute turned up in my e-mail box. On page 9 "recreation" and "neighborhood sporting clubs" appear in the list of mechanisms leading to good health. These are not my words, but just the same, they are welcome as signs that, in the eyes of researchers at this Institute, leisure does figure in the formula for mental and, possibly, physical well-being.
3. Having no time for leisure is, as the years go by, becoming a less convincing excuse for not participating in any free time activity, except the most hedonic and easily available casual leisure. At least three recent issues of the *Economist* (2003; 2004; 2005b) have described general trends toward fewer hours of work in OECD countries, in general, and Britain and the United States, in particular. Still, nonwork obligations could be consuming a significant portion of the newfound time away from work.

References

Adler, P., and Adler, P. (1987). *Membership roles in field research*. Beverly Hills, CA: Sage.

Adorjánÿ, L., and Lovejoy, F., 2003. Representations of leisure in the writings of Robert G. Barrett. *Annals of leisure research*, 6 (4), 307-318.

Aitchison, C. (2003). From leisure and disability to disability leisure: Developing data, definitions, and discourses. *Disability and Society*, 18, 955-969.

Apostle, R. (1992). Curling for cash: The "professionalization" of a popular Canadian sport. *Culture*, 12(2), 17-28.

Arai, S.M. (2000). Typology of volunteers for a changing sociopolitical context: The impact on social capital, citizenship, and civil society. *Société et Loisir/Society and Leisure*, 23, 327-352.

Baldwin, C.K., and Norris, P.A. (1999). Exploring the dimensions of serious leisure: Love me—love my dog. *Journal of Leisure Research*, 31, 1-17.

Bartram, S.A. (2001). Serious leisure careers among whitewater kayakers: A feminist perspective, *World Leisure Journal*, 43(2), 4-11.

Bates, M.J. (1999). The invisible substrate of information science. *Journal of the American Society for Information Science*, 50(12), 1043-1050.

Beauchesne, E. (2005). Hate you job? You're not alone. *Calgary Herald* (Friday, 2 September), p. E6.

Beck, U. (2000). *The brave new world of work,* trans. by P. Camiller. New York: Polity Press.

Becker, H.S. (1960). Notes on the concept of commitment. *American Journal of Sociology*, 66, 32-40.

Belbin, L. (2003). The opt-out revolution. *New York Times Magazine* (Sunday 26 October), pp. 1-13.

Bella, L. (1992). *The Christmas imperative: Leisure, family, and women's work*. Halifax, NS: Fernwood.

Benoit, J., and Perkins, K.B. (1997). Volunteer fire-fighting activity in North America as serious leisure. *World Leisure and Recreation,* 39(3), 23-29.

Blackshaw, T., and Long, J. (1998). A critical examination of the advantages of investigating community and leisure from a social network perspective. *Leisure Studies*, 17, 233-248.

Blumer, H. (1969). *Symbolic interactionism*. Englewood Cliffs, NJ: Prentice-Hall.

Bott, E. (1957). *Family and social network*. London, UK: Tavistock Publications.

Bowen, C.D. (1935). *Friends and fiddlers*. Boston, MA: Little Brown.

Bramante, A.C. (2004). Fostering human resources in the leisure field: "Serious leisure" and the potential role of volunteers. A proposal for developing countries. In R. A. Stebbins, and M. M. Graham (Eds.), *Volunteering as leisure/leisure as volunteering: An international assessment* (pp. 225-240). Wallingford, Oxon, UK: CAB International.

Brightbill, C.K. (1961). *Man and leisure: A philosophy of recreation.* Englewood Cliffs, NJ: Prentice-Hall.

Bryan, H. (1977). Leisure value systems and recreational specialization: The case of trout fishermen. *Journal of Leisure Research,* 9, 174-187.

Burden, J. (2000). Community building, volunteering, and action research. *Société et Loisir/Society and Leisure,* 23, 353-370.

Burden, J. (2001). Volunteering, citizenship and action research. In M. Graham and M. Foley (Eds.), *Volunteering in leisure: Marginal or inclusive?* vol. 75 (pp. 21-42). Eastbourne, UK: Leisure Studies Association.

Bush, D.M., and Simmons, R.G. (1990). Socialization processes over the life course. In M. Rosenberg and R.H. Turner (Eds.), *Social Psychology* (pp. 133-164). New Brunswick, NJ: Transaction Publishers.

Campbell, A., Converse, P., and Rogers, W.L. (1976). *The quality of American life: Perceptions, evaluations, and satisfactions.* New York: Russell Sage Foundation.

Cantwell, A-M. (2003). Deviant leisure. In J.M. Jenkins and J.J. Pigram (Eds.), *Encyclopedia of leisure and outdoor recreation* (p. 114). London: Routledge.

Cassie, L.T., and Halpenny, E. (2003). Volunteering for nature: Leisure motivations and benefits associated with a biodiversity conservation volunteer program. *World Leisure Journal,* 45(2), 38-50.

Cnaan, R.A., Handy, F., and Wadsworth, M. (1996). Defining who is a volunteer: Conceptual and empirical considerations. *Nonprofit and Voluntary Sector Quarterly,* 25, 364-383.

Codina, N. (1999). Tendencias emergentes en el comportamiento de ocio: El ocio serio y su evaluación. *Revista de Psicología Social,* 14, 331-346.

Cohen-Gewerc, E., and Stebbins, R.A. (Eds.) (in press). *The pivotal role of leisure education: Finding personal-fulfillment in this century.* State College, PA: Venture.

Crawford, D.W., and Godbey, G. (1987). Reconceptualizing barriers to family leisure. *Leisure Sciences,* 9, 119-127.

Cross, G. (1990). *A social history of leisure since 1600.* State College, PA: Venture.

Csikszentmihalyi, M. (1990). *Flow: The psychology of optimal experience.* New York, NY: Harper and Row.

Cuskelly, G., Harrington, M., and Stebbins, R.A. (2002/2003). Changing levels of organizational commitment amongst sport volunteers: A serious leisure approach. *Leisure/Loisir,* 27, 191-212.

de Grazia, S. (1962). *Of time, work, and leisure.* New York: Twentieth Century Fund.

Delbaere, R. (1994). Le tourisme culturel et récréotouristique, leurs approches méthodologiques et leurs potentialités. Paper presented at the International Leisure Studies Conference, Université du Québec à Trois-Rivières, Trois-Rivières, Québec, 3-4 November.

Drew, R.S. (1997). Embracing the role of amateur: How karaoke bar patrons become regular performers. *Journal of Contemporary Ethnography,* 25, 449-468.

Driver, B. (2003). Benefits. In J.M. Jenkins and J.J. Pigram (Eds.), *Encyclopedia of leisure and outdoor recreation* (pp. 31-36). London: Routledge.

Dubin, R. (1992). *Central life interests: Creative individualism in a complex world.* New Brunswick, NJ: Transaction Publishers.

The Economist (2003). Clocking off. 19 July, pp. 43-44.

The Economist (2004). Working hours (graph). 21 August, p. 80.

The Economist (2005a). Up off the couch. 22 October, p. 35.

The Economist (2005b). The land of pleasure. 4 February, pp. 28-29.

Edwards, D. (2005). Understanding the organization of volunteers at visitor attractions. Ph.D. dissertation, College of Law and Business, University of West Sydney.

Etheridge, M., and Neapolitan, J. (1985). Amateur craft-workers: Marginal roles in a marginal art world. *Sociological Spectrum*, 5, 53-76.

Fine, G.A. (1988). Dying for a Laugh. *Western Folklore*, 47, 77-194.

Floro, G.K. (1978). What to look for in a study of the volunteer in the work world. In R.P. Wolensky and E.J. Miller (Eds.), *The small city and regional community* (pp. 194-202). Stevens Point, WI: Foundation Press.

Gelber, S.M. (1999). *Hobbies: Leisure and the culture of work in America*. New York: Columbia University Press.

Gibson, H., Willming, C., and Holdnak, A. (2002). We're gators...not just Gator fans: Serious leisure and University of Florida football. *Journal of Leisure Research*, 34, 397-425.

Gillespie, D.L., Leffler, A., and Lerner, E. (2002). If it weren't my hobby, I'd have a life: Dog sports, serious leisure, and boundary negotiations. *Leisure Studies*, 21, 285-304.

Glaser, B.G. (1978). *Theoretical sensitivity: Advances in the methodology of grounded theory*. Mill Valley, CA: Sociology Press.

Glaser, B. G., and Strauss, A.L. (1967). *The Discovery of grounded theory: Strategies for qualitative research*. Chicago, IL: Aldine Atherton.

Glasser, R. (1970). *Leisure: Penalty or prize?* London: Macmillan.

Goff, S.J., Fick, D.S., and Oppliger, R.A. (1997). The moderating effect of spouse support on the relation between serious leisure and spouses' perceived leisure-family conflict. *Journal of Leisure Research*, 29, 47-60.

Goffman, E. (1961). *Asylums: Essays on the social situation of mental patients and other inmates*. Garden City, NY: Doubleday.

Goffman, E. (1963). *Stigma: Notes on the management of spoiled identity*. Englewood Cliffs, NJ: Prentice-Hall.

Gould, J., Moore, D., and Stebbins, R.A. (in press). Development of the Serious Leisure Inventory and Measure. *Journal of Leisure Research*.

Graham, M.M. (2004). Volunteering as heritage/volunteering in heritage. In R. A. Stebbins, and M. M. Graham (Eds.), *Volunteering as leisure/leisure as volunteering: An international assessment* (pp. 13-30). Wallingford, Oxon, UK: CAB International.

Gravelle, F., and Larocque, L. (2005). Volunteerism and serious leisure: The case of the francophone games. *World Leisure Journal*, 47(1), 45-51.

Green, B.C., and Chalip, L. (2004). Paths to volunteer commitment: Lessons from the Sydney Olympic Games. In R. A. Stebbins, and M. M. Graham (Eds.), *Volunteering as leisure/leisure as volunteering: An international assessment* (pp. 49-68). Wallingford, Oxon, UK: CAB International.

Gunter, G.B., and Gunter, N.C. (1980). Leisure styles: A conceptual framework for modern leisure. *The Sociological Quarterly*, 21, 361-374.

Hall, C. M, and Weiler, B. (1992). Introduction. What's special about special interest tourism. In B. Weiler and C.M. Hall (eds.), *Special interest tourism* (pp. 1-14). New York: Wiley.

Halpern, D. (2005). *Social capital*. Cambridge: Polity.

Hamilton-Smith, E. (1995). The connexions of scholarship. *Newsletter* (Official newsletter of RC13 of the International Sociological Association), March, 4-9.

Harries, G.D., and Currie, R.R. (1998). Cognitive dissonance: A consequence of serious leisure. *World Leisure and Recreation*, 40(3), 36-41.

Harrington, M., Cuskelly, G., and Auld, C. (2001). Career volunteering in commodity-intensive serious leisure: Motorsport events and their dependence on volunteers/amateurs. *Société et Loisir/Society and Leisure*, 23, 327-352.

Harrison, J. (2001). Thinking about tourists. *International Sociology*, 16, 159-172.1

Hartel, J. (2003). The serious leisure frontier in library and information science: hobby domains. *Knowledge organization*, 30(3/4), 228-238.

Hastings, D.W., and Cable, S. (2005). The globalization of a minor sport: The diffusion and commodification of masters swimming. *Sociological Spectrum*, 25, 133-154.

Hastings, D.W., Kurth, S.B., and Schloder, M. (1996). Work routines in the serious leisure career of Canadian and U.S. masters swimmers. *Avanté*, 2, 73-92.

Hastings, D.W., Kurth, S.B., Schloder, M., and Cyr, Darrell (1995). Reasons for participating in a serious leisure: Comparison of Canadian and U.S. masters swimmers. *International Review for Sociology of Sport* 30, 101-119.

Havighurst, R.J., and Feigenbaum, K. (1959). Leisure and life-style. *American Journal of Sociology*, 64, 396-404.

Haworth, J.T. (1986). Meaningful activity and psychological models of non-employment. *Leisure Studies*, 5, 281-297.

Haworth, J.T. (Ed.) (1997). *Work, Leisure and Well-Being*. London: Routledge.

Haworth, J.T., and Drucker, J. (1991). Psychological well-being and access to categories of experience in unemployed young adults. *Leisure Studies*, 10, 265-274.

Haworth, J.T., and Hill, S. (1992). Work, leisure, and psychological well-being in a sample of young adults. *Journal of Community and Applied Social Psychology*, 2, 147-160.

Henderson, K.A., and Presley, J. (2003). Globalization and the values of volunteering as leisure. *World Leisure Journal*, 45(2), 33-37.

Heuser, L. (2005). We're not too old to play sports: The career of women lawn bowlers. *Leisure Studies*, 24, 45-60.

Houle, C.O. (1961). *The inquiring mind*. Madison: University of Wisconsin Press.

Hunt, S.J. (2004). Acting the part: "Living history" as a serious leisure pursuit. *Leisure Studies*, 23, 387-404.

Hutchinson, S.L., and Kleiber, D.A. (2005). Gifts of the ordinary: Casual leisure's contributions to health and well-being. *World Leisure Journal*, 47(3), 2-16.

Iso-Ahola, S.E., and Crowley, E.D. (1991). Adolescent substance abuse and leisure boredom. *Journal of Leisure Research*, 23, 260-271.

Jarvis, P. (1995). *Adult and continuing education*, 2nd ed. London, Eng.: Routledge.

Jarvis, N., and King, L. (1997). Volunteers in uniformed youth organizations. *World Leisure & Recreation*, 39 (3), 6-10.

Jones, I. (2000). A model of serious leisure identification: The case of football fandom. *Leisure Studies*, 19, 283-298.

Jones, I., and Symon, G. (2001). Lifelong learning as serious leisure: Policy, practice, and potential. *Leisure Studies*, 20, 269-284.

Jung, B. (2005). Poland. In G. Cushman, A.J. Veal, and J. Zuzanek (Eds.), *Free time and leisure participation: International perspectives* (pp. 197-220). Wallingford, Oxon, U.K.: CAB International.

Juniu, S., and Henderson, K. (2001). Problems in researching leisure and women: Global considerations. *World Leisure Journal*, 43(4), 3-10.

Juniu, S., Tedrick, T., and Boyd, R. (1996). Leisure or work? Amateur and professional musicians' perception of rehearsal and performance. *Journal of Leisure Research*, 28, 44-56.

Kando, T.M. (1980). *Leisure and popular culture in transition*, 2nd ed. St. Louis, MO: C.V. Mosby.

Kane, M.J., and Zink, R. (2004). Package adventure tours: Markers in serious leisure. *Leisure Studies*, 23, 329-346.

Kantor, R.M. (1968). Commitment and social organization. *American Sociological Review*, 33, 499-517.

Kaplan, M. (1960). *Leisure in America: A social inquiry.* New York: John Wiley.

Kaplan, M. (1975). *Leisure: Theory and policy.* New York: John Wiley

Katz, J. (1988). *Seductions of crime: Moral and sensual attractions of doing evil.* New York: Basic Books.

Kelly, J.R. (1997). Activity and ageing: Challenge in retirement. In J.T. Haworth (Ed.), *Work, leisure and well-being* (pp. 165-179). London, UK: Routledge.

Kelly, J. R. (1999). Leisure behaviors and styles: Social, economic, and cultural factors. In E.L. Jackson and T.L. Burton (Eds.), *Leisure studies: Prospects for the twenty-first century* (pp. 135-150). State College, PA: Venture.

Kennett, B. (2002). Language learners as cultural tourists. *Annals of Tourism Research,* 29, 557-559.

Kerr, J.H., Fujiyama, H., and Campano, J. (2002). Emotion and stress in serious and hedonistic leisure sport activities. *Journal of Leisure Research,* 34, 272-289.

Keyes, C.L.M. (1998). Social well-being. *Social Psychology Quarterly,* 61, 121-140.

King, F.L. (2001). Social dynamics of quilting, *World Leisure Journal,* 43(2), 26-29.

Kleiber, D.A. (1996) (July). Personal expressiveness and the transcendence of negative life events. Paper presented at the 4th World Congress of Leisure Research, World Leisure and Recreation Association, Cardiff, Wales.

Kleiber, D.A. (2000). The neglect of relaxation. *Journal of Leisure Research,* 32, 82-86.

Lambdin, L. (1997). *Elderlearning.* Phoenix, AZ: Oryx Press.

Lambert, R.D. (1995). Looking for genealogical motivation. *Families,* 34, 73-80.

Lambert, R.D. (1996). Doing family history. *Families,* 35, 11-25.

Lee, J-Y, and Scott, D. (2006). For better or worse? A structural model of the benefits and costs associated with recreational specialization. *Leisure Sciences,* 28, 17-38.

Lee, Y., Dattilo, J., and Howard, D. (1994). The complex and dynamic nature of leisure experience. *Journal of Leisure Research,* 26, 195-211.

Lee, Y., McCormick, B., and Austin, D. (2001). Toward an engagement in social support: A key to community integration in rehabilitation. *World Leisure Journal,* 43(3), 25-30.

Maffesoli, M. (1996). *The time of the tribes: The decline of individualism,* trans. by D. Smith. London, UK: Sage Publications.

Major, W.F. (2001). The benefits and costs or serious running, *World Leisure Journal,* 43(2), 12-25.

Mannell, R.C. (1993). High investment activity and life satisfaction among older adults: Committed, serious leisure, and flow activities. In J.R. Kelly (Ed.), *Activity and aging: Staying involved in later life* (pp.125-145). Newbury Park, CA: Sage.

Mannell, R.C. (1999). Leisure experience and satisfaction. In E.L. Jackson and T.L. Burton (Eds.), *Leisure studies: Prospects for the twenty-first century* (pp. 235-252). State College, PA: Venture.

Mannell, R.C., and Kleiber, D.A. (1997). *A social psychology of leisure.* State College, PA: Venture.

Matejko, A.J. (1984). The self-defeat of leisure: The macro-social model and its application, *Sociologia Internationalis,* 22, 161-196.

McIntyre, N. (2003). Involvement. In J.M. Jenkins and J.J. Pigram (Eds.), *Encyclopedia of leisure and outdoor recreation* (pp. 268-270). London: Routledge.

McQuarrie, F.A.E. (1999). An investigation of the effects of workplace support for serious leisure. *Proceedings of the 9th Canadian Congress on Leisure Research.* Wolfville, NS: Acadia University.

McQuarrie, F.A.E. (2000). Work careers and serious leisure: The effects of nonwork commitment on career commitment. *Leisure/Loisir,* 24, 115-138.

McQuarrie, F., and Jackson, E.L. (1996). Connections between negotiation of leisure constraints and serious leisure: An exploratory study of adult amateur ice skaters. *Loisir et Société/Society and Leisure*, 19, 459-483.

Mittelstaedt, R.D. (1990-91). The Civil War reenactment: A growing trend in creative leisure behavior. *Leisure Information Quarterly*, 17(4), 4-6.

Mittelstaedt, R.D. (1995). Reenacting the American Civil War: A unique form of serious leisure for adults. *World Leisure and Recreation*, 37(1), 23-27.

Olmsted, A.D. (1988). Morally controversial leisure: The social world of the gun collector. *Symbolic Interaction*, 11, 277-287.

Olmsted, A.D. (1991). Collecting: Leisure investment or obsession? *Journal of Social Behavior and Personality*, 6, 287-306.

Olmsted, A.D. (1993). Hobbies and serious leisure. *World Leisure and Recreation*, 35 (Spring), 27-32.

Orr, N. (2003). Heritage and leisure: Museum volunteering as "serious leisure." In R. Snape, E. Thwaites, and C. Williams (Eds.), *Access and inclusion in leisure and tourism* (Vol. 81, pp. 119-140). Brighton, UK: Leisure Studies Association.

Orr, N. (2005). "A giving culture": Understanding the rewards from volunteering in museums." *Leisure Studies Association Newsletter*, 71(July), 43-48.

Parker, S.R. (1996). Serious leisure—A middle-class phenomenon? In M. Collins (Ed.), *Leisure in industrial and post-industrial societies* (pp. 327-332). Eastbourne, UK: Leisure Studies Association.

Patterson, I. (1997). Serious leisure as an alternative to a work career for people with disabilities. *Australian Disability Review*, 2, 20-27.

Patterson, I. (2000). Developing a meaningful identity for people with disabilities through serious leisure activities. *World Leisure Journal*, 42(2), 41-51.

Patterson, I. (2001). Serious leisure as a positive contributor to social inclusion for people with intellectual disabilities. *World Leisure Journal*, 43(3), 16-24.

Pearce, J.L. (1993). *Volunteers: The organizational behavior of unpaid workers*, London, UK: Routledge.

Perkins, K.B., and Benoit, J., (2004). Volunteer satisfaction and serious leisure in rural fire departments: Implications for human capital and social capital. In R. A. Stebbins, and M. M. Graham (Eds.), *Volunteering as leisure/leisure as volunteering: An international assessment* (pp. 71-86). Wallingford, Oxon, UK: CAB International.

Polson, G. (2006). Leisure alternatives funnel chart. http://www.strengthtech.com/misc/funnel/funnel.htm.

Pringle, R. (2001). Examining the justifications for government investment in high performance sport: A critical review essay. *Annals of Leisure Research*, 4, 58-75.

Puddephatt, A.J. (2003). Chess playing as strategic activity. *Symbolic Interaction*, 26, 263-284.

Puddephatt, A.J. (2005). Advancing in the amateur chess world. In D. Pawluch, W. Shaffir, and C. Miall (Eds.), *Doing ethnography: Studying everyday life* (pp. 300-311). Toronto, ON: Canadian Scholars' Press.

Putnam, R.D. (2000). *Bowling alone: The collapse and revival of American community*. New York: Simon and Schuster.

Raisborough, J. (1999). Research note: The concept of serious leisure and women's experiences of the Sea Cadet Corps. *Leisure Studies*, 18, 67-72.

Roadburg, A. (1985). *Aging: Retirement, leisure, and work in Canada*. Toronto, ON: Methuen.

Roberson, D.N., Jr. (2005). Leisure and learning: An investigation of older adults and self-directed learning. *Leisure/Loisir*, 29, 203-238.

Robinson, J.P., and Godbey G. (1997). *Time for life: The surprising ways Americans use their time*. University Park, PA: Pennsylvania State University Press.

Rojek, C. (1997). Leisure theory: Retrospect and prospect. *Loisir et Société/Society and Leisure*, 20, 383-400.

Rojek, C. (1999). Deviant leisure: the dark side of free-time activity. In E.L. Jackson and T.L. Burton (Eds.), *Leisure studies: Prospects for the twenty-first century* (pp. 81-96). State College, PA: Venture.

Rojek. C. (2000). *Leisure and culture*. London: Palgrave.

Rojek, C. (2002). Civil labour, leisure and post work society. *Société et Loisir/Society and Leisure*, 25, 21-36.

Rojek, C. (2005). *Leisure theory: Principles and practice*. New York: Palgrave Macmillan.

Ruskin, H., and Sivan, A. (1995). Goals, objectives, and strategies in school curricula in leisure education. In H. Ruskin, and A. Sivan (Eds.), *Leisure education towards the 21st century*. Provo, UT: Brigham Young University.

Ruskin, H., and Sivan, A. (n.d.). *Leisure education in school systems*. Jerusalem, IS: Cosell Center for Physical Education, Leisure, and Health Promotion, The Hebrew University of Jerusalem.

Samdahl, D.M. (1999). Epistemological and methodological issues in leisure research. In E.L. Jackson, and T.L. Burton (Eds.), *Leisure studies: Prospects for the twenty-first century* (pp. 119-134). State College, PA: Venture.

Scott, D. (2003). Constraints. In J.M. Jenkins and J.J. Pigram (Eds.), *Encyclopedia of leisure and outdoor recreation* (pp. 75-78). London: Routledge.

Scott, D., and Godbey, G.C. (1992). An analysis of adult play groups: Social versus serious participation in contract bridge. *Leisure Sciences*, 14, 47-67.

Scott, D., and Godbey, G.C. (1994). Recreation specialization in the social world of contract bridge. *Journal of Leisure Research*, 26, 275-295.

Scott, D., and Schafer, C.S. (2001). Recreational specialization: A critical look at the construct. *Journal of Leisure Research*, 33, 319-343.

Selman, G., Selman, M., Cooke, M., and Dampier, P. (1998). *The foundations of adult education in Canada*, 2nd ed. Toronto, ON: Thompson.

Shaw, S.M., and Dawson, D. (2001). Purposive leisure: Examining parental discourses on family activities. *Leisure Sciences*, 23, 217-232.

Sheykhi, M.T. (2003) A general review of the conceptual dimensions of quality of leisure, tourism, and sports with a particular focus on Iran, *African and Asian Studies*, 2, 189-206.

Shinew, K.J., and Parry, D.C. (2005). Examining college students' participation in the leisure pursuits of drinking and illegal drug use. *Journal of Leisure Research*, 37, 364-387.

Siegenthaler, K.L., and Gonsalez, G.L. (1997). Youth sports as serious leisure: A critique. *Journal of Sport and Social Issues*, 21, 298-314.

Siegenthaler, K.L., and O'Dell, I. (2003). Older golfers: Serious leisure and successful aging. *World Leisure Journal*, 45(1), 45-52.

Smith, D.H. (2000). *Grassroots associations*. Thousand Oaks, CA: Sage Publications.

Smith, D.H., Stebbins, R.A., and M. Dover (2006). *A dictionary of nonprofit terms and concepts*. Bloomington: Indiana University Press.

Snyder, E.E. (1986). The social world of shuffleboard: Participation among senior citizens. *Urban Life*, 15, 237-53.

Stebbins, R.A. (1970a). Career: The subjective approach. *Sociological Quarterly*, 11, 32-49.

Stebbins, R.A. (1970b). On misunderstanding the concept of commitment: A theoretical clarification. *Social Forces*, 48 (4), 526-529.

Stebbins, R.A. (1976). Music among friends: The social networks of amateur musicians. *International Review of Sociology* (Series II), 12, 52-73.

Stebbins, R.A. (1978a). Amateurism and postretirement years. *Journal of Physical Education and Recreation (Leisure Today* supplement), 49 (October), 40-41.

Stebbins, R.A. (1978b). Classical music amateurs: A definitional study, *Humboldt Journal of Social Relations*, 5, 78-103.

Stebbins, R.A. (1978c). Creating high culture: The American amateur classical musician, *Journal of American Culture*, 1, 616-631.

Stebbins, R.A. (1979). *Amateurs: On the margin between work and leisure*. Beverly Hills, CA: Sage.

Stebbins, R.A. (1980a). "Amateur" and "hobbyist" as concepts for the study of leisure problems. *Social Problems*, 27, 413-417.

Stebbins, R.A. (1980b). Avocational science: The amateur routine in archaeology and astronomy, *International Journal of Comparative Sociology*, 21, 34-48.

Stebbins, R.A. (1981a). The social psychology of selfishness. *Canadian Review of Sociology and Anthropology*, 18, 82-92.

Stebbins, R.A. (1981b). Toward a social psychology of stage fright. In M. Hart and S. Birrell (Eds.), *Sport in the sociocultural process* (pp. 156-163). Dubuque, IA: W.C. Brown.

Stebbins, R.A. (1982a). Serious leisure: A conceptual statement. *Pacific Sociological Review*, 25, 251-272.

Stebbins, R.A. (1982b). Amateur and professional astronomers: A study of their interrelationships. *Urban Life*, 10, 433-454.

Stebbins, R.A. (1990). *The laugh-makers: Stand-up comedy as art, business, and lifestyle*. Montréal, QC and Kingston, ON: McGill-Queen's University Press.

Stebbins, R.A. (1992a). *Amateurs, professionals, and serious leisure*. Montreal, QC and Kingston, ON: McGill-Queen's University Press.

Stebbins, R.A. (1992b). Concatenated exploration: Notes on a neglected type of longitudinal research. *Quality and Quantity*, 26, 435-442.

Stebbins, R.A. (1993a). *Career, culture and social psychology in a variety art: The magician* (reprinted ed.). Malabar, FL: Krieger.

Stebbins, R.A. (1993b). *Predicaments: Moral difficulty in everyday life*. Lanham, MD: University Press of America.

Stebbins, R.A. (1993c). *Canadian football. A view from the helmet.* (reprinted ed.). Toronto, ON: Canadian Scholars Press.

Stebbins, R.A. (1994a). The liberal arts hobbies: A neglected subtype of serious leisure. *Loisir et Société/Society and Leisure*,16, 173-186.

Stebbins, R.A. (1994b). *The Franco-Calgarians: French language, leisure, and linguistic lifestyle in an anglophone city*. Toronto, ON: University of Toronto Press.

Stebbins, R.A. (1995a). *The connoisseur's New Orleans*. Calgary, AB: University of Calgary Press.

Stebbins, R.A. (1995b). Leisure and selfishness: An exploration. In G. S. Fain (Ed.), *Reflections on the philosophy of leisure, Vol. II, Leisure and ethics* (pp. 292-303). Reston, VA: American Alliance for Health, Physical Education, Recreation, and Dance.

Stebbins, R.A. (1996a). *The barbershop singer: Inside the social world of a musical hobby*. Toronto, ON: University of Toronto Press.

Stebbins, R.A. (1996b). Volunteering: A serious leisure perspective. *Nonprofit and Voluntary Action Quarterly*, 25, 211-224.

Stebbins, R.A. (1996c). Cultural tourism as serious leisure. *Annals of Tourism Research*, 23, 948-950.

Stebbins, R.A. (1996d). *Tolerable differences: Living with deviance* (2nd ed.). Toronto, ON: McGraw-Hill Ryerson.

Stebbins, R.A. (1996e). Casual and serious leisure and post-traditional thought in the information age. *World Leisure and Recreation*, 38(3), 4-11.

Stebbins, R.A. (1997a). Casual leisure: A conceptual statement. *Leisure Studies*, 16, 17-25.

Stebbins, R.A. (1997b). Lifestyle as a generic concept in ethnographic research. *Quality and Quantity*, 31, 347-360.

Stebbins, R.A. (Ed.) (1997c). *World Leisure and Recreation* (special issue on volunteerism and the leisure perspective), 39(3), 3-33.

Stebbins, R.A. (1997d). Exploratory research as an antidote to theoretical stagnation in leisure studies. *Loisir et Société/Society and Leisure*, 20, 421-434.

Stebbins, R.A. (1997e). Identity and cultural tourism. *Annals of Tourism Research*, 24, 450-452.

Stebbins, R.A. (1997f). Serious leisure and well-being. In J.T. Haworth (Ed.), *Work, Leisure and Well-Being* (pp. 117-130). London: Routledge.

Stebbins, R.A. (1998a). *After work: The search for an optimal leisure lifestyle*. Calgary, AB: Detselig.

Stebbins, R.A. (1998b). Of time and serious leisure in the information age: The case of the Netherlands. *Vrijetijdstudies*, 16, 19-32.

Stebbins, R.A. (1998c). Serious leisure and wayward youth. Paper presented at the Youth at Risk Seminar of the Leisure Education Commission of the World Leisure and Recreation Association, Northeastern Mexico University, Monterrey, October.

Stebbins, R.A. (1998d). *The urban francophone volunteer: Searching for personal meaning and community growth in a linguistic minority*. Vol. 3, No. 2 (New Scholars-New Visions in Canadian Studies quarterly monographs series). Seattle, WA: University of Washington, Canadian Studies Centre.

Stebbins, R.A. (1999). Educating for serious leisure: Leisure education in theory and Practice. *World Leisure and Recreation*, 41(4), 14-19.

Stebbins , R. A. (2000a). Optimal leisure lifestyle: Combining serious and casual leisure for personal well-being. In M. C. Cabeza (Ed.), *Leisure and human development: Proposals for the 6th World Leisure Congress*. (pp. 101-107). Bilbao, Spain: University of Deusto.

Stebbins, R.A. (2000b). Obligation as an aspect of leisure experience. *Journal of Leisure Research*, 32, 152-155.

Stebbins, R.A. (2000c). Antinomies in volunteering: choice/obligation, leisure/work. *Société et Loisir/Society and Leisure*, 23, 313-326.

Stebbins, R.A. (2000d). The extraprofessional life: Leisure, retirement, and unemployment. *Current Sociology*, 48, 1-27.

Stebbins, R.A. (2000e). A contextual analysis of the idea of serious leisure: A Study in the sociology of knowledge. *World Leisure and Recreation*, 42(1), 4-9.

Stebbins, R.A. (2001a). *New directions in the theory and research of serious leisure*, Mellen Studies in Sociology, vol. 28. Lewiston, NY: Edwin Mellen.

Stebbins, R.A. (2001b). The costs and benefits of hedonism: Some consequences of taking casual leisure seriously. *Leisure Studies*, 20, 305-309.

Stebbins, R. A. (2001c). *Exploratory research in the social sciences*. Thousand Oaks, CA: Sage.

Stebbins, R. A. (2001d). Volunteering—mainstream and marginal: Preserving the leisure experience. In M. Graham and M. Foley (Eds.), *Volunteering in leisure: Marginal or inclusive?* (Vol. 75, pp. 1-10). Eastbourne, UK: Leisure Studies Association.

Stebbins, R. A. (2002). *The organizational basis of leisure participation: A motivational exploration*. State College, PA: Venture Publishing.

Stebbins, R.A. (2003a). Boredom in free time. *Leisure Studies Association Newsletter*, 64 (March), 29-31.

Stebbins, R.A. (2003b). Casual leisure. In J.M. Jenkins and J.J. Pigram (Eds.), *Encyclopedia of leisure and outdoor recreation* (pp. 44-46). London: Routledge.

Stebbins, R.A. (2004a). Introduction. In R. A. Stebbins, and M. M. Graham (Eds.), *Volunteering as leisure/leisure as volunteering: An international assessment* (pp. 1-12). Wallingford, Oxon, UK: CAB International.

Stebbins, R.A. (2004b). *Between work and leisure: The common ground of two separate worlds*. New Brunswick, NJ: Transaction Publishers.

Stebbins, R.A. (2004c). Serious leisure, volunteerism, and quality of life. In J. Haworth and T. Veal (Eds.), *The future of work and leisure* (pp. 200-212). London: Routledge.

Stebbins, R.A. (2004d). Fun, enjoyable, satisfying, fulfilling: Describing positive leisure experience. *Leisure Studies Association Newsletter*, 69 (November), 8-11

Stebbins, R.A. (2004e). Pleasurable aerobic activity: A type of casual leisure with salubrious implications. *World Leisure Journal*, 46(4), 55-58.

Stebbins, R.A. (2005a). Project-based leisure: Theoretical neglect of a common use of free time. *Leisure Studies*, 24, 1-11.

Stebbins, R.A. (2005b). Choice and experiential definitions of leisure. *Leisure Sciences*, 27, 349-352.

Stebbins, R.A. (2005c). *Challenging mountain nature: Risk, motive, and lifestyle in three hobbyist sports*. Calgary, AB: Detselig.

Stebbins, R.A. (2005d). Inclination to participate in organized serious leisure: An exploration of the role of costs, rewards, and lifestyle. *Leisure/Loisir*, 29, 181-199.

Stebbins, R.A. (2005e). The role of leisure in arts administration. *Occasional Paper Series*, Paper No. 1. Eugene, OR: Center for Community Arts and Public Policy, University of Oregon. (published online at: http://aad.uoregon.edu/icas/documents/stebbins0305.pdf)

Stebbins, R.A. (2005f). On the importance of concepts in leisure studies. *Leisure Studies Association Newsletter*, 71, 32-35.

Stebbins, R.A. (2005g). Serious leisure, recreational specialization, and complex leisure activity. *Leisure Studies Association Newsletter*, 70, 11-13.

Stebbins, R.A. (2006a). Shopping as leisure, obligation, and community. *Leisure/Loisir*, 30,

Stebbins, R.A. (2006b). Concatenated exploration: Aiding theoretic memory by planning well for the future. *Journal of Contemporary Ethnography*, 35,

Stebbins, R.A. (2006c). Leisure and popular culture. In G. Ritzer (Ed.), *The Blackwell Encyclopedia of the Social Sciences* (pp. 21-23). Cambridge, MA: Blackwell.

Stebbins, R.A. (2006d). Contemplation as leisure and nonleisure. *Leisure Studies Association Newsletter*, 73, pp.

Stebbins, R.A. (2006e). Leisure Lifestyles. In R.E. McCarville and K.J. MacKay (Eds.), *Leisure for Canadians* (pp. 21-23). State College, PA: Venture.

Stebbins, R.A. (in press). The sociology of entertainment. In C.D. Bryant and D.L. Peck (Eds), *The Handbook of 21st Century Sociology*. Thousand Oaks, CA: Sage.

Stokowski, P.A. (1994). *Leisure in society: A network structural perspective*. New York: Mansell Publishing.

Storr, M. (2003). *Latex and lingerie: Shopping for pleasure at Ann Summers Parties*. Oxford, UK: Berg.

Thompson, M.C. (1997a). *Volunteer firefighters: Our silent heroes*. Unpublished doctoral dissertation, Department of Sociology, University of Calgary.

Thompson, M.C. (1997b). Employment-based volunteering: Leisure or not? *World Leisure and Recreation* 39(3), 30-33.

Todd, E. (1930). Amateur. In R.A. Seligman (Ed.), *Encyclopedia of the Social Sciences*, vol. 2 (pp. 18-20). New York: Macmillan.

Tompkins, J. (2003). Flight 737 now departing from your garage. *New York Times* (Thurs, 25 Sept.), http://www.nytimes.com/2003...pilo.html.

Tomlinson, A. (1993). Culture of commitment in leisure: Notes towards the understanding of a serious legacy. *World Leisure and Recreation* 35(1), 6-9.

Truzzi, M. (1972). The occult revival as popular culture. *Sociological Quarterly*, 13, 16-36.

Twynam, G.D., Farrell, J.M., and Johnston, M.E. (2002/2003). Leisure and volunteer motivation at a special sporting event. *Leisure/Loisir*, 27, 363-377.

UNESCO. (1976). Recommendation on the development of adult education. Paris, France.

Unruh, D.R. (1979). Characteristics and types of participation in social worlds. *Symbolic Interaction*, 2, 115-130.

Unruh, D.R. (1980). The nature of social worlds. *Pacific Sociological Review*, 23, 271-296.

Urry, J. (1994). Cultural change and contemporary tourism. *Leisure Studies*, 13, 233-238.

VandeSchoot, L. (2005). Navigating the divide: Muslim perspectives on Western conceptualizations of leisure. Masters Thesis, Wageningen University, Social Spatial Analysis Chair Group.

Veal, A.J. (1993). The concept of lifestyle: A review. *Leisure Studies*, 12, 233-252.

Wearing, S.L. (2001). *Volunteer tourism: Seeking experiences that make a difference.* Wallingford, Oxon, UK: CAB International.

Wearing, S.L. (2004). Examining best practice in volunteer tourism. In R. A. Stebbins, and M. M. Graham (Eds.), *Volunteering as leisure/leisure as volunteering: An international assessment* (pp. 209-224). Wallingford, Oxon, UK: CAB International.

Wearing, S.L., and Neil, J. (2001). Expanding sustainable tourism's conceptualization: Ecotourism, volunteerism, and serious leisure. In S.F. McCool, and R.N. Moisey (Eds.), *Tourism, recreation and sustainability* (pp. 233-254). Wallingford, Oxon, UK: CAB International.

Williams, R.M., Jr. (2000). American society. In E.F. Borgatta, and R.J.V. Montgomery (Eds.), *Encyclopedia of sociology*, 2nd ed., Vol. 1 (pp. 140-148). New York: Macmillan.

Wilson, K. (1995). Olympians or lemmings? The postmodernist fun run. *Leisure Studies*, 14, 174-185.

Yair, G. (1990). The commitment to long-distance running and level of activities. *Journal of Leisure Research*, 22, 213-227.

Yair. G. (1992). What keeps them running? The "circle of commitment" of long distance runners. *Leisure Studies*, 11, 257-270.

Yarnal, C.M., and Dowler, L. (2002/2003). Who is answering the call? Volunteer firefighting as serious leisure. *Leisure/Loisir*, 27, 161-190.

Yedes, J., Clamons, K., and Osman, A. (2004). Buna: Oromo women gathering for coffee. *Journal of Contemporary Ethnography*, 33, 675-703.

Yoder, D.G. (1997). A model for commodity intensive serious leisure. *Journal of Leisure Research*, 29, 407-429.

Index